MW01164835

A DOER SELLER'S GUIDE FOR BEING SUCCESSFUL AT SALES

A Doer Seller is an individual within any vertical market in any size company who is expected to deliver a quality product or service or is expected to manage a group of people or manage a business practice and, at the same time, is expected to deliver the revenue dollars associated with sales goal or quota in a timely manner, along with his or her other responsibilities

HOWARD DION

In every vertical market, sales organizations compete one against the other based on how effective they are in running the same five sales management practices.

Copyright © 2011 Howard Dion
All rights reserved.
ISBN: 1463753349
ISBN 13: 9781463753344
Library of Congress Control Number: 2011913084
CreateSpace, North Charleston, SC

CONTENTS

PREFACE

My wife read the title of this book and, before reading the introduction, said, "What is a Doer Seller?" I thought that was a legitimate question and agreed that other readers might want clarification as well.

If it weren't for my recent clients, I would not have recognized the role of a Doer Seller and how difficult and demanding the job really is. For that insight, I would like to say thank you. I'd like to take this a step further with a formal definition that you can add to your glossary of terms.

DOER SELLER: *A Doer Seller is an individual within any vertical market in any size company who is expected to deliver a quality product or service or is expected to manage a group of people or manage a business practice and, at the same time, is expected to deliver the revenue dollars associated with a sales goal or quota in a timely manner, along with their other responsibilities.*

There are some very significant challenges associated with this job description, and I hope that this book will address some or all of the challenges. Obviously, my focus is on the sales side of the Doer Seller role.

There is one point of clarification that I would like to make in recognition of those who actually fulfill the opposite role. In most instances, especially in professional service firms, the term frequently used is Seller Doer. This job function is also a reality. The individual's primary job function is to sell, and their secondary job function is to do something else. However, what I learned from working with companies that actually employ these roles was that the majority are in reality Doer

Sellers. A project manager in a technology company who was expected to sell did project management first and then sales. An engineer who was expected to design something did that first and then found new clients. A market research practitioner who was expected to sell sold the project, then delivered the project, and then went back to the role of sales. Architects, lawyers, and accountants can also be Doer Sellers. Successful Doer Sellers in any industry also have another title; they are called "rainmakers."

This book is also for the entrepreneurs of the world. People like me. I own my own business, Matrix Consulting Group, LLC, and have no employees. I do 100% of the sales and deliver what I sell. I also do all the bookkeeping and design of my deliverables. When I had my other training company, Dynamic Learning Systems, Inc., I had a couple of salespeople and was still a Doer Seller. I sold my services to different companies, as did the salespeople, and then did all the delivery of the training programs myself.

Howard Dion

INTRODUCTION

After ten years of being in business for myself, I decided to write a book about my experience. Prior to this business, I owned two other businesses and in between was vice president of sales for a financial services firm, sold technical training in the information technology sector, and sold sales training to large public and private companies.

The reason for writing this book is straightforward. Now that I am reaching retirement age, I want to share my thinking and what I have learned over the years. This is something that I would never have considered doing earlier in my career.

This book is about sales processes and about managing those processes. It is about adopting a common sales language to make communication more efficient and more effective. This is especially important considering we live in a global marketplace where we must interact with different cultures. Process is about taking something through a standardized set of procedures to convert it from one form to another form; for example, turning a preliminary sales meeting into a quote, and then into a sale. Process is about discipline and being able to clearly identify a step that does not work and being able to change that step so that it does work. When a sales training company delivers a training program for its particular sales methodology, it is delivering a process: a standardized set of operating procedures that gets an identified result the majority of the time when you follow the process.

As I started to write this book and think about the people I have worked with over the years, I made an important discovery. I recognized a personal success driver, the thing behind the process that made certain individuals very successful in sales. The discovery was this: *Some people have a love for what they do for a living. They have an absolute passion for the work that manifests itself as a dedicated and unwavering use of whatever sales process they had adopted.*

Over the last ten years, I have worked with thirty-six different companies in five different vertical markets. I personally touched the lives of over 263 human beings. I worked with people up and down the corporate value chain with every imaginable title. To all of these people, I owe a debt of gratitude and am thankful that I had an opportunity to know each and every person on a first-name basis.

In closing this introduction, I would like to give recognition to those I was influenced by but cannot specifically identify as contributors to my personal success. Most important, I would like to thank all the Doer Sellers and Seller Doers who make important contributions to the world of business and who are sometimes unappreciated for their work ethic. Long live the entrepreneurial spirit!

CHAPTER 1—GETTING STARTED

THE DOER SELLER ROLE

The majority of clients I worked with employed Doer Sellers. They were the people expected to design and/or deliver a product or service and, at the same time, were expected to bring in new clients and continue to grow sales revenue from existing clients.

The Doer Seller role has no boundaries. The role crosses different vertical markets and is not distinct to only a certain size company. Employees in any size company who are asked to serve both roles are Doer Sellers. People who go into business for themselves and have no employees are also Doer Sellers. A person's formal job title is not a key indicator of the Doer Seller role. The role thrives in the background, below the surface, and is an engine that sustains and drives ongoing revenue streams.

There are some really tough challenges associated with being successful at serving two masters, your primary job function and your secondary job function. What makes the role of a Doer Seller even more difficult is when priorities shift back and forth; when senior management applies pressure on the employee to focus on sales when sales is the secondary job function. Below are some of the challenges that I will address in this book.

1. Seeing sales from a professional perspective that empowers the individual to respect the seller role as much as the doer role by understanding the thinking behind

what constitutes successful Sales Management Practices and Sales Opportunity Practices.

2.   Understanding the benefits of using formal processes for new business development, Key Account management, and strategic selling for complex sales opportunities.

3.   Understanding the importance of managing a formal sales pipeline, including the statistics that offer the user an opportunity to improve performance results.

4.   Having the insight to better manage sales meetings to obtain results that serve the needs of both the buyer and the seller.

5.   Having the insight to better manage time and internal and external resources that are associated with closing a sale.

6.   Having the insight to overcome the most common sales problems associated with today's complicated sales environment.

7.   Offering those with no direct sales management experience an opportunity to excel in managing the sales end of the Doer Seller equation.

The above list is not prioritized. From my personal experience, all of these things are equally important and must be adopted by the Doer Seller to varying degrees depending on the intensity of the organization's management practices. My intention is to make all of these challenges easy to overcome and to master, so that the Doer Seller can live with less stress and still be highly successful in both roles. The trigger, as always, is careful planning and execution.

From this point forward the term "seller" is synonymous with the Doer Seller role and the role of the professional salesperson.

ATTITUDE

An attitude is a habit of thinking, just like eating and sleeping are habits. Attitude is the number one place to begin when starting a business, becoming a professional salesperson, living the life of a Doer Seller, or managing a group of these professionals. Attitudes manifest themselves as behaviors and fall into two categories: positive and negative. There is no middle of the road, no ambivalent attitude. In order to define an attitude as positive or negative, there must be an object on which an attitude is focused. These objects can be words, ideas, activities, events, places, things, people, and experiences. You can have a good experience, which would then be reflected as a good attitude, which in turn would impact your future behavior. Unfortunately, the opposite is also true. An attitude toward a particular object is reflected in a behavior that produces a specific result, which we then define as good or bad.

Going into business for myself for a third time was a challenge. Would I be successful or would I fail? I decided to form some new work habits which I realized would need to start with some new ways of thinking. So I looked into my personal "attitude mirror" and made the following changes:

❖ Micromanaging myself needed to be a positive, so I designed a tracking system that would generate the statistics I needed to monitor and improve my performance. This Scorecard system allowed me to manage myself. As a footnote, my self-management system later became an Insight Tool that I used with all of my clients.

❖ Working from a home office was the same as working in an office filled with people. Again, the right attitude was

3

critical. Shave, shower, and get dressed before you go to work.

❖ Having something of value to offer prospective clients needed to be a belief that motivated me to action. In other words, I believe in my ability (My Attitude) to sell my products, and services (The Objects), which motivates me to make outbound calls (My Behavior) that gets me a sales meeting so I can close a sale (The Result).

ATTITUDES AND THE DOER SELLER/PROFESSIONAL SALESPERSON

This process is easy to understand; it is not complicated. Keeping in mind that the word "positive" means helpful and upbeat and the word "negative" means harmful or downbeat, here is a list of twelve important objects that Doer Sellers, professional salespeople, and their managers need to check in their "personal attitude mirror." And, they need to do this task objectively and in writing. Put a date on the document so you can refer back to the original attitude test from time to time. Keep in mind that your attitude (habit of thinking) is either positive or negative, which impacts how you behave, which in turn equals a specific result. Circle the numbers that you would categorize as negative.

1. Your employer

2. Your manager

3. Your manager's manager

4. The products and services you sell

5. The people who deliver the products and services you sell

6. The sales process used for new business development

7. Corporate support for new business development (marketing)

8. The sales process used to manage Key Accounts

9. Other members of your team

10. A family member's view of your employer and your job

11. Your own view about making a living as a Doer Seller, salesperson, or as a manager

12. The space you work in

Next, examine the circled, negative numbers. First look at the reasons behind the negative attitude. Chances are they are based on some past experience. If that is true, put those experiences aside and start over, focusing on your current situation. If the negative thoughts come from other people, what they say and/or what they do, then negotiate; talk to the individual impacting your attitude. The truth is you have total control of how you think and behave and little or no control over how others think or behave. However, as a seller you have the power of influence. Use the skill!

All of this thinking and self-reflection has two possible outcomes. First, you could get excited and motivated and want to take action. When that happens, use an electronic calendar and start scheduling the time required to accomplish whatever needs to get done. Second, you could also feel anxious and become filled with self-doubt. When that is the outcome, you will start to worry and feel uneasy with what you must accomplish. If and when that happens, use a worry list.

USING A WORRY LIST

I was working with a client in Australia who had no dedicated sales team. My interactions were by telephone conference calls and, of course, e-mail and the Internet. Of the four Doer Sellers that I coached for the client, all four were extremely dedicated to making sales while delivering what they were originally hired to deliver. There were, of course, cultural differences that I needed to overcome in order to successfully communicate my ideas. In the third year of our relationship, something very interesting occurred. One of my contacts was given an additional role in one of the client's vertical markets, which added time to his already busy work schedule. My contact started to worry and reached out to me for help. We created what we called a Legitimate Worry List. Of the twenty-three worries originally listed, we decided to pass twelve on to those employees who were actually responsible for the issue. We then decided on an action plan for each of the remaining eleven worries. Not only was my contact grateful for the solution, he in turn decided to use the idea with one of his direct reports.

Worrying is a time killer and a drain on your emotional energy. Our attitudes, the way we think, and what we think about sometimes manifest into what is called a worry, and worries keep us awake at night. So here's a suggestion that I have used personally and recommended to others that really worked for them as well. When you recognize that you are in a worrying mode, use a worry list.

- ❖ Get a package of three-by-five cards, and write one worry on each card.

- ❖ When finished, review the worries to make sure the responsibility for them all belongs to you.

❖ Give the ones that don't belong to you to the person who really owns the worry. (Many times we worry about things that are not ours to worry about.)

❖ Review the cards periodically and throw away the cards that represent a worry that took care of itself, which is what happens the majority of the time.

❖ Put the remaining cards in your desk or your briefcase.

❖ When anxiety overcomes you, take the cards out, read them, add any new worries that have surfaced, throw away the worries that are no longer valid, and put the cards back in your desk or briefcase.

The three-by-five cards will be there for you any time you want to review your personal worry list.

From a sales perspective, there is a good side to the human mind plague called worrying. Worrying is a negative to the person with the worry and a positive for the seller attempting to make the sale. If I, the seller, can discover what is keeping you, the buyer, awake at night and can offer a cost-effective solution that will make the worry disappear, I will have a high probability of closing the sale. This concept is implemented by asking the right questions to the right people.

Understanding where you are in the value chain versus where you need to be in the value chain is critically important to ongoing sales success. There is more content around this topic later in the book. For now, here is a guide that you may find helpful. Asking the right kind of open-ended questions to people in the following roles can have amazing results.

Executive Role	Functional Manager Role	Line Manager Role
•Governs corporate resources, assesses business problems, and defines acceptable solution metrics	•Governs the buying process, evaluates solution options, and establishes the ground rules for buyer/seller interaction	•Governs the proposal process, selects vendors, and negotiates delivery and pricing options

MOTIVATION

Consider this statement: *motivation is the reason human beings take action, and the reasons behind the actions can come from within the individual or from some external source, like another human being.* There has been a significant amount of research done on the subject of motivation, and I am by no means an expert on the topic. What I offer here are my personal observations based on a sales perspective. There are four types of motivation, and each has advantages and disadvantages depending on the circumstances.

Fear Motivation	Incentive Motivation	Power Motivation	Attitude Motivation

Sellers must know, and the emphasis is on *must know*, what personally motivates a buyer. Sales managers must know what motivates their direct reports. Having this knowledge allows us to link to, and then capitalize on, the motivating factor. Below are some examples of how each motivating factor might manifest itself as a reason or purpose to take action, or in some cases not to take action.

❖ **Fear Motivation**

✓ Fear of Rejection

✓ Fear of Failure

✓ Fear of Success

❖ **Incentive Motivation**

✓ Personal Recognition

✓ Organizational Recognition

✓ Job Security

✓ Financial Security

❖ **Power Motivation**

✓ Ego Gratification

✓ Power and Control

✓ The Ability to Influence People or Outcomes

✓ A Job Title

❖ **Attitude Motivation**

✓ Personal or Corporate Values

✓ A Person's Perception of Something

✓ What a Person Thinks About

✓ A Desired Result or Outcome

Using fear motivation to manage people has a negative impact on corporate culture, as that type of motivation is a detriment to a value-driven work ethic, innovation, and creativity. Selling to an individual who is motivated by fear of failure is a challenging task. The decision-making process is always negatively impacted when the individual is driven by fear.

Using incentive motivation to manage people or to incent a buyer to make a decision in your favor always has financial barriers that limit sales success.

Using power motivation is dangerous and can have negative side effects. You, as the seller, can get sidetracked or derailed in your sales effort by political infighting within the client's organization.

Attitude motivation has the most impact and longevity. Using this method requires an ability to ask open-ended questions that reveal what a person thinks about so you can identify and meet his or her personal and business needs, wants, and desires.

THE CONCEPT OF SALES PRACTICES

In business a practice represents a product or service where people repeatedly use their competencies to deliver a valuable outcome to an end-user. To gain market share, vendors compete for dollars, pitting business practice against business practice. Here's an example: The ABC Company designs and manufactures medical devices. It has an Injection Molding Practice, a Urethane Castings Practice, and a Rapid Tooling Practice. Other competitors who have the same practices constantly compete against the ABC Company for business in the same vertical market.

The same is true for sales organizations. In every vertical market, sales organizations compete one against the other based on the same five Sales Management Practices and the same four Sales Opportunity Practices.

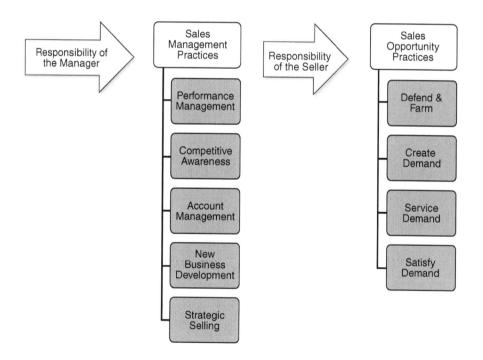

The challenge for the Doer Seller is that all the practices fall on his or her shoulders. Understanding what each practice signifies and how they link together simplifies the challenge. Defining a sales process that supports each practice is also a required component of successful implementation. If these ideas become how the Doer Seller thinks, then the behavior that follows creates a more successful work environment.

CHAPTER 2—SALES MANAGEMENT PRACTICES

PERFORMANCE MANAGEMENT PRACTICES

What is the sales leader responsible for? The answer to that question seems to change from organization to organization. Clearly, the sales leader is responsible for the overall performance of the sales team under his or her control. But what specifically must the individual do to fulfill the role of sales leader? I think it's critical to mention that it's not the title that's important; it's the role that is important. "Vice president of sales," "director of sales," "regional sales manager," and just plain old "sales manager" all fall into the sales leader bucket. Therefore, the following rules of play apply to all, regardless of title. If you are responsible for leading sales, I recommend you do the following:

❖ **Rule #1: Establish metrics that are used to manage and coach the performance of employees who share responsibility for sales.**

✓ **Pipeline Win Rate** reflects the behavior of the seller and can be used for forecasting. The Win Rate goes up when sales dollars are closed, and the Win Rate goes down when new dollars are added to the active sales pipeline. The Win Rate does not change when an opportunity is lost. The Win Rate starts at zero at the beginning of the year, slowly climbs to the 20% or 30% range, and then levels off with only minor fluctuations. Exceptionally high Win Rates (over 40%) or exceptionally low Win Rates (less than 20%) are a red flag. The calculation looks like this:

Active dollars in the pipeline (business development and proposals)	$500,000
Business sold	$150,000
Business lost	$75,000
Total Pipeline	**$725,000**
Win Rate = (business sold of $150,000 ÷ the total pipeline of $725,000) x 100	21%

✓ **Proposal Decision Rate** is commonly called "Closing Rate." This metric reflects the selling or closing skills of the individual. An average target Decision Rate is between 50% and 65% for business-to-business sales. The calculation looks like this:

Number of YES decisions by the client	17
Number of NO decisions by the client	15
Total Decisions	**32**
Decision Rate = (YES decisions of 17 ÷ by the total decisions of 32) x 100)	53%

✓ **Meeting Conversion Rate** is an important metric that very few people measure. How many sales meetings must I hold on the phone or in person to get to the proposal stage? Technical meetings after the proposal is delivered do not count in this metric.

✓ **Average Deal Size Won and Average Deal Size Lost.** If I am managing or coaching a salesperson and see his or her average Deal Size Lost is significantly higher than his or her average Deal Size Won, we have a challenge to overcome. I have worked with some really high-powered professional salespeople and the differences between the two are usually minimal. If there is a significant difference, higher than 20%, investigate!

❖ **Rule #2: Utilize a formal Customer Relationship Management or CRM-driven sales pipeline process.** The report layout is important but could be limited by the software vendor and/or the consulting company supporting the software vendor. I have worked with clients using Microsoft Dynamics CRM, Salesforce. com, Sage SalesLogix, and with individuals using an Excel pipeline worksheet designed by me. Just entering data into the CRM doesn't mean anything unless there are reports coming out of the CRM that empower the sellers and the sales leader to monitor and improve their performance. One last critically important point. You can and should mandate that your people be diligent in using the CRM. From my experience, if the salesperson gains some personal benefit from using the CRM, he or she will be more motivated to be diligent in using the CRM. On the next page is an example of what I mean. Look at the information that is generated. There are benefits in knowing exactly what needs to be accomplished to meet or exceed quota.

EXAMPLE OF CRM REPORT

KPI Tracking	Actual YTD	Targets	Variance
Sales Dollars	$4,875	$40,543	$(35,668)
Pipeline Win Rate	19%	48%	(29%)
Proposal Decision Rate	67%	65%	2%
Average Size Deals Won	$2,438	$3,459	$(1,021)
Pipeline Management			
Total Sales Pipeline YTD	$26,075		
Amount Required to Hit Target Based on Actual Win Rate	$216,853		
Variance	$(190,778)		
Number of Deals Required to Hit KPI Target	17		
Number of Deals Actually Closed	2		
Variance	(15)		
Average Probability Forecast	64%		
Average Size Deals Lost	$4,575		
Revenue Forecast			
Amount Active in Pipeline	$16,625		
Win Rate Forecast	$3,108		
Probability % Forecast	$10,688		
Percent of YTD Quota	12%		

❖ **Rule #3: Run sales pipeline meetings weekly, preferably early Monday morning, and utilize a**

written agenda and a report generated from the CRM. The agenda can change from time to time but should include:

✓ What was closed since the last meeting?

✓ What was lost since the last meeting, and why was it lost?

✓ What was added to the pipeline since the last meeting?

✓ Review the CRM report representing the deals which have: (a) an expected decision date on or before the current month and (b) a 50% or greater probability of closing.

❖ **Rule #4: Clearly define and communicate the individual's roles and responsibilities.** A written job description is critical, as that is the only way to avoid misunderstandings. I recommend the employee write the job description with guidance and final approval from his or her manager. For me, a job description must contain these five sections:

1. **Accountability:** What business functions do you own? What are you liable for to your employer?

2. **Responsibility:** What is the proper sphere or extent of your activities within each area of accountability?

3. **Authority to Act:** Concerning your areas of accountability, when must you seek approval from your manager before taking action?

4. **Measurement Criteria:** What will you measure in order to manage your responsibilities? Targets

can then be transferred to the performance review process.

5. **Reporting Criteria:** What reports are you required to complete by a specific deadline? What information must you maintain? What technologies are you required to use in your position?

❖ **Rule #5: Complete weekly or bi-weekly one-on-one coaching sessions.** This is a critical management component that allows for coaching and for feedback from a direct report. Scheduling those thirty to forty-five minute time slots allows for reinforcement of whatever sales methodology your company has adopted. Companies spend millions of dollars on sales training each year, and that training fades in a matter of weeks without continued reinforcement. There are really only two choices senior management can make and each has a different result.

	Choice #1	End Result	Choice #2	End Result
Use of Formal Sales Process by Salespeople	Not Considered a Priority by Senior Management	Everybody Still Does His or Her Own Thing	Utilization is Mandated by Senior Management	Usage Becomes a Cultural Norm

❖ **Rule #6: Conduct quarterly performance reviews.** Waiting until the end of the year to complete a performance review leaves no time for setting performance improvement goals or professional development goals. Consider using your one-on-one coaching time (see Rule #5) to do the performance review. I designed a performance review format called CPAS, Co-developed Performance Appraisal System. The idea is to establish and agree to both objective and subjective feedback systems. For more details, see the CPAS example on page 24.

Usually, the Doer Seller does not serve two masters. In other words, he or she does not report to both a practice manager and a sales leader. With that in mind, I'd like to review the six rules of performance management practices and articulate how they impact the daily life of the Doer Seller.

- ❖ **Rule #1: Establish metrics that are used to manage and coach the performance of employees who share responsibility for sales.** This knowledge is critical for the Doer Seller. Knowing the numbers allows for more accurate planning and saves time. Knowing just how many sales meetings are needed to get the required number of proposals on the table that will lead to getting the required number of closed sales goes a long way in reducing the stress associated with having a sales quota.

- ❖ **Rule #2: Utilize a formal CRM-driven sales pipeline process.** Again, a critical must-do. Managing an active pipeline on a daily or weekly basis keeps the Doer Seller focused on sales when project delivery or managing people or managing a practice is the number one priority in the effective use of time.

- ❖ **Rule #3: Run sales pipeline meetings weekly, preferably early Monday morning, and utilize a written agenda and a report generated from the CRM.** The Doer Seller should attend the pipeline sales meetings, especially if the meetings target a vertical market which is the Doer Seller's area of expertise. Knowing what other sellers are doing is usually a very enlightening experience.

❖ **Rule #4: Clearly define and communicate the individual's roles and responsibilities.** This is a necessity for the Doer Seller because the process is a means to an end. Outcomes become realistic when both the manager and the Doer Seller agree on performance expectations.

❖ **Rule #5: Complete weekly or bi-weekly one-on-one coaching.** This rule is most critical. A Doer Seller is not a professional salesperson who makes their living solely from sales. When the Doer Seller has a good sales process coach, then there is a much higher probability of sales success. From personal experience as a sales process coach, I've learned keeping the Doer Seller motivated and being there to help solve sales problems reduces stress and makes a difference from a revenue-generating perspective.

❖ **Rule #6: Conduct quarterly performance reviews.** A welcome methodology designed to align expectations and encourage adjustments in thinking and behavior.

Once upon a time there was a Doer who become a Doer Seller and then became just a Seller. She went through this transformation in less than eighteen months. Unfortunately, she never had any formal sales training prior to moving to the Seller role. As her sales coach, I had to command her to use my strategic selling process. She was extremely tenacious and goal-driven, but the idea of sitting down and spending time thinking about strategy and tactics made her resistant to the recommendation. She just wanted to use her fifteen years of Doer experience to close the sale.

I had a conversation with her many months later, after I had stopped working with her one-on-one as her sales coach. The company had brought in a different sales training company, and she went through that training as well. No surprises, she still verbalized her resistance to using a formal sales process as part of her daily routine. After some discussion about her recent sales activity, I had a personal *aha*. She used neither my structured sales process nor the other company's sales process on a regular basis. Yet from both she had adopted the thinking, the question-asking techniques, and the behaviors associated with using a strategic sales process. The repeated exposure to the concepts during the training and adoption cycles had changed her behavior. She had become a "product of the product" without recognizing her own professional growth.

CPAS EXAMPLE

I recommended that one of my clients start utilizing a performance appraisal system for its sales staff. The owner asked me about different options, and after some discussion on alternatives, we agreed that CPAS was a good choice. The only problem was that the owner did not want to commit the time to the process and asked me if I would be willing to commit the time. Since I was already engaged with the sales team under an annual contract, I agreed. For two years, once per quarter, I met with each salesperson one-on-one to complete the performance appraisal process. Doing CPAS reviews on a quarterly basis soon become a customary expectation. The salespeople looked forward to the meetings because of the professional development goals. When they were on track, they liked the personal recognition. When they were off track, it was an opportunity to get some coaching support. As it turned out, the owner liked the CPAS process, too, and linked the annual performance objectives and year-to-date stats into the CRM. The weekly report that disclosed everyone's numbers offered a sense of control to the owner so that there were no surprises at the end of the year! There were five people on the team, and only one was a Doer Seller.

Part I: Measurable Performance Standards

(Recommend Five Objective Performance Criteria)

Measurable Performance Goals or Key Performance Indicators (KPIs)	Annual Expectation Range	Q1	Q2	Q3	Q4	YTD Stats
Annual Target #1						

Part II: Employee Self-Assessment Report to Management Q1

(Recommend the Same Questions Each Quarter)

Sample Questions	Employee Feedback
1. Briefly describe the work accomplished on your performance goals or KPIs during this period.	
2. What will you focus on during the next period?	
3. What challenges do you anticipate for the next period, and how will you overcome those challenges?	
4. What recommendations can you make that will improve your performance or the performance of others in the organization?	

Part III: Professional Development Plan of Action Q1

(Recommend Four Goals per Quarter)

Goal #1		Goal #2	
Action Steps:		Action Steps:	
Measure:		Measure:	
Target Date:		Target Date:	
End of Period Result:		End of Period Result:	

Part IV: Manager Feedback

Area	Manager Comments	Ratings
Part I: Measurable Performance Standards		
Part II: Employee Self-Assessment Report to Management		
Part III: Professional Development Assessment and Plan of Action		

Ratings: 1=Unsatisfactory, 2=Needs Improvement, 3=Satisfactory, 4=Exceeds Expectation, 5=Significantly Exceeds Expectation

COMPETITIVE PRACTICES

To some organizations, the idea of actually managing competitive strategies and tactics is a complete unknown. To other organizations, it is a way of life. Competitive Practices start with how you define and sell your company's business value. I found this to be a problem with most of the sales organizations I worked with. Sellers simply had difficulty in defining their business value. How Competitive Practices get managed impacts everyone on the client-facing team: the people who deliver the product or service, the Doer Sellers, and the full-time salespeople. The most impact may be with the senior management team, since they interact with the marketplace in general and make decisions that impact the client-facing team.

My solution came from the process of building a Tactical Playbook. I will offer more details concerning the playbook in Chapter 4. We completed all three modules in a day; I took the workbooks completed by the client back to the office and wrote the formal document. Then we scheduled a second meeting to tweak the content. The final step was deciding how to best utilize the outcomes. Problem solved! Below is an outline of the process.

Module #1—Positioning

❖ Write a positioning statement so all those on the client-facing team agree about how they want to be perceived by their internal or external customers. This perception refers to the position you desire to hold in people's minds. There can and should be different positioning strategies for different vertical markets.

❖ Define affirming and undermining behaviors in writing so that expectations are clear concerning how those behaviors impact how you want to be perceived. Managers and employees now have a tool to better self-govern their behavior.

Module #2—Strategy

❖ Clearly define your competencies to better understand the engine that is your business. This empowers your sales team to more easily articulate and sell your business value.

❖ Clearly define your Key Performance Indicators (KPIs) so you can measure and improve your competency performance. This makes it possible for you to set and achieve meaningful benchmarks that align with overall corporate strategy.

❖ Complete a matrix that links competencies to KPIs. Evaluate and set performance improvement goals.

❖ Write preliminary value propositions by vertical market. This allows your sales team to own a method that effectively communicates your business value to prospective clients.

Module #3—Tactics

❖ Develop talking points so you can improve communications at all levels of the value chain. At the same time this will empower the organization's sales staff (full-time salespeople and Doer Sellers) to develop Allies and Sponsors who will use their influence on your behalf.

❖ Develop value statements and probing questions so staff can better sell your business value, test for and obtain competitive intelligence, and determine which competencies are most critical to which client contacts.

❖ Develop inoculation messages that can be used preemptively to offset misperceptions about your organization and the competitive tactics of aggressive competitors.

❖ Build a Competitive Game Plan. I recommend defining ten to twelve core competencies. Then assign the task of defining one or two competencies to each workshop participant. In essence you build a glossary of terms that *clearly defines your business value*. From there you can build an Insight Tool that looks like this:

Who is your most dangerous competitor?					
COMPETENCY RATING: A=Strong, B=Moderate, C=Weak, D=Unknown **EXCLUSIVITY RATING:** A=Exclusive to your organization, B=Exclusive to the competitor, C=Shared **IMPORTANCE RATING:** A=Critical, B=Important, C=Useful **YOUR COMPETITIVE GAME PLAN:** 1=Emphasize, 2=Deemphasize, 3=Value Probe, 4=Inoculate, 5=Ignore					
List Your Competencies Below:	Rate Your Organization	Rate the Competitor	Exclusivity Rating	Client Importance Rating	Your Competitive Game Plan

From my experience, this is where self-discipline becomes a factor. It takes about fifteen minutes to think through this Insight Tool. Knowing the names of the vendors you are competing against during any particular strategic sales opportunity is critical. If it is a transactional sales opportunity, there is no reason to spend time on this process. On page 31 is a model that illustrates the difference between the two types of sales opportunities.

Asking questions to obtain competitive intelligence early in the sales cycle must become a way of life if you want to improve your decision rates and gain increased market share. The easiest way to develop Allies and Sponsors is by being really good at relationship development.

An Ally will use his or her personal influence to favor the seller. A Sponsor uses his or her political power to help the seller meet the right people up and down the value chain. A Primary Sponsor uses his or her authority to gain access to required resources, such as time, people, and money.

There are also questions that need to be asked, and there is a less threatening way to ask those questions. Instead of asking a direct question like, "Who am I competing against?" you could ask, "From your perspective, what do you like and what do you dislike about the vendors bidding on this work? What are their strengths and weaknesses?" Ask open-ended questions. Once they start talking, the competitors' names will inevitably be disclosed. Better yet, call a current client Ally and ask for competitive intelligence about other vendors he or she has worked with in the past. In the final analysis, it is not just the companies who are competing, but also a salesperson from Company A competing against a salesperson from Company B. Remember this point: *Sellers do not control product, price, or industry presence. They control how they sell!*

Strategic vs. Transactional Sales Model

One day in early spring, I did a workshop for a group of Doers. The motivation behind the workshop was two new corporate objectives. First, assess which people in the group could become Doer Sellers, and second, educate everyone in the room about sales process so they could better support the full-time sales team. We started promptly at 9:00 a.m. and finished at 4:00 p.m. At that point, the president asked for feedback from the participants. The overall feedback was generally positive. But then something really unexpected happened. One long-term employee stood up and said, "If I have to work on transactional sales along with my other duties, you'll have my resignation first thing in the morning." The president responded quickly. "How about strategic selling?" he asked. "Strategic selling is okay, but none of that transactional stuff," the employee replied. With that he sat down and the entire room exploded with applause.

	Transactional Sales		Strategic Sales	
Type of Buyer	❖ Commodity Buyer (Owns the Task)	❖ Product Buyer (Owns the Project)	❖ Solution Buyer (Owns the Problem)	❖ Consultancy Buyer (Owns the Strategy)
Business Relationship	❖ Vendor on Demand	❖ State-of-the-Art Product and/or Service Provider	❖ Business Problem Solving Counselor	❖ Long-Range Planning Partner
Personal Relationships	❖ Casual	❖ Built on Trust and Mutual Rapport	❖ Influence Oriented (Political*)	❖ Partnering Oriented (Political*)
Seller's Focus	❖ Take the Order	❖ Identify and Meet Current Needs and Close the Sale	❖ Eliminate the Competition	❖ Drive Ongoing Revenue Streams
Authority to Act	❖ Limited to the Task at Hand	❖ Report Up the Value Chain and Then Act	❖ Based on Budget Resources	❖ Self-Directed
Formal Sales Process	❖ Not Required	❖ Required for Complex Sales**	❖ Required for Complex Sales**	❖ Required for Complex Sales**
Sales Timeline	❖ Immediate to 90 Days (Maybe 120 Days)		❖ 3 Months to a Year (Maybe More)	

* "Political" is intended to have a positive connotation concerning social relationships involving personal influence, authority, and power.

** A Complex Sale has a sales cycle lasting three months to a year and has multiple decision makers controlling the buying process

Account Management Practices

Although Key Account management is a priority in every company, the process is generally handled in a haphazard fashion. There are two important factors concerning Key Account management: the process used to differentiate Key Accounts from Secondary Accounts and Tertiary Accounts, and the process used to grow profitable revenue streams within Key Accounts.

For me, a Key Account is an objective term. In other words, a Key Account has the potential to drive significant revenue streams around a particular product or service, regardless of which vendor currently "owns the account." Usually, salespeople and Doer Sellers make Key Account decisions based on how much revenue they are driving from specific accounts. From my perspective, this is flawed thinking because it eliminates other vendors' Key Accounts from our vision. Below are ten questions that should be answered in order to objectively assign the term "Key Account" to a company you are currently doing business with, or an account you may be targeting from a business development perspective. Each yes answer equals ten points, so the higher the score, the more inclined I am to agree that the account is indeed Key!

1. Does this account have multiple lines of business and/ or multiple locations that have the potential to generate business based on what you are selling?

2. If your company had favored vendor status, could this account generate significant revenue streams over the next three to five years?

3. From a vertical market perspective, is this account strategically important to your company?

4. Does this account have a history of using the kinds of products and services that your company provides?

5. Does the economy currently favor this account's vertical market?

6. Are you competitively advantaged when competing for business in this account's vertical market?

7. Have you been able to develop Allies high in the account's value chain? If not, do you believe you can develop Allies high in the value chain over the next twelve months?

8. Do you have a Sponsor or Primary Sponsor supporting your sales effort? If not, do you believe you can obtain sponsorship over the next twelve months?

9. Does the account have the potential to meet your revenue projection over the next twelve months?

10. If you lost this account, for whatever reason, would the loss have a major impact on your reputation and/or personal income?

You don't have to agree with my ten questions; you can create questions of your own. The point is, do not leave Key Account selection to a subjective decision-making process. Apply your limited resources to where you can get the greatest Return on Investment (ROI).

What does a formal Key Account management process look like? My answer to that question is, "*a repeatable information-based process that forces the user to think and then act in an organized manner to achieve specific goals and objectives.*" I designed two different workbooks specifically for account management: the Key Account Sales Plan and the Strategic Ownership Account Plan. There were three versions of the Key Account Sales Plan. The original version targeted one account. That evolved to a version that allowed an account team of four people to work together on one account or for one account owner to use one workbook to manage four different accounts. The final version was simplified and was vertical-market focused. I will illustrate an outline of the three versions and will then go into more detail about the Strategic Ownership Account Plan. The Strategic Ownership Account Plan, which I called SOAP, was designed for Doer Sellers who value their time above all else.

The Key Account Sales Plans

2004 Version (20 Pages)	2006 Version (24 Pages)	2010 Version (10 Pages)
❖ Recommended Meeting Review Cycle	❖ Top Ten Revenue Forecast	❖ Strategy
❖ Understanding the Customer's Business Environment	➤ Revenue Forecast— Top Four Accounts	➤ Vertical Market Analysis
❖ Determine Account Potential	❖ Team Plan of Action	➤ Six Sales Strategy Questions
➤ Logistics Map	➤ Vertical Market Analysis	➤ Buying Process Map
➤ Formal/Informal Decision-Making Map	➤ Buying Process Map	➤ Sales History
➤ Account Potential Worksheet	➤ Sales History by Account or by Salesperson	❖ Tactics
❖ Acquisition Worksheet	➤ Business Penetration by Account or by Salesperson	➤ Business Penetration Map
❖ Primary Plan of Action	➤ Relationship Development by Account or by Salesperson	➤ Nonrevenue Relationship Planner
❖ Annual Sales Projection	➤ Success Stories	➤ Meeting Planner (Face-to-Face Only)
❖ Nonrevenue Relationship Planner	➤ Account or Salesperson Meeting Planner, #1, #2, #3, #4 (Face-to-Face Only)	➤ Vertical Market Influence Planner
❖ Nonrevenue Influence Planner		➤ Customer Success Stories
❖ Annual Meeting Planner for Key Contacts	❖ Status Report	➤ Revenue Forecast
❖ Account Goal Setting Program	➤ The First 30 Days	❖ Status Report
➤ Master Dream List	➤ The First 3 Months	➤ Plan of Action
➤ 30-Day Follow-Up Work in Progress List	➤ The First 6 Months	
❖ Sales Meeting Planner	➤ The First 9 Months	
	➤ Year-End	

The Strategic Ownership Account Plan (SOAP)

I was working with a group of salespeople and a group of Doer Sellers in the same company. The vice president of sales asked me to work on delivering a formal account management process that would help everyone improve upon an already successful part of the business. A significant part of their annual revenue came from existing clients. The client would buy the service and then renew the program year after year. Since the client base was made up of very large companies with a global presence, the challenge was in infiltrating other business units and geographic locations where the competition owned the account.

I set up a one-day workshop with the salespeople and delivered the Key Account Sales Plan (KASP) using existing accounts. By lunchtime it became apparent to me that I would need to deliver a different process to the Doer Sellers, because they would never commit their time to this information-intensive, complex account management process. My solution was to deliver the simplified, but no less effective, Strategic Account Sales Plan (SOAP) to the Doer Sellers. The irony was that the Doer Sellers already had more of the required information at their fingertips simply because of their onsite working environment and relationship dynamics. From a one-on-one coaching perspective, SOAP reduced my time commitment from two-plus hours for a KASP down to thirty to forty-five minutes for SOAP. The interesting part of this experience was that the Doer Sellers were much less resistant to adopting a formal account management process than were the professional salespeople. In the first six months of adoption, several people, Doer Sellers and salespeople, had infiltrated several different geographic locations and knocked out the competition.

The first page of SOAP is like a sign-in sheet. It asks for the account name, the date range of the plan, and the name of the person taking ownership of the plan. Next, and this is important, I ask for two lists: (1) All the names and titles of people that touch the account from inside the company, and (2) All the names and titles of people that touch this account from outside the company. These lists are used to develop a Plan of Action.

The next thing we do is look at high payoff activities. Below are the instructions to completing the exercise. For whatever reason, sellers struggle with articulating their top five high payoff activities. They usually get one or two and then must really stop and think. Of course, this is one of my primary objectives: to get sellers to stop and think about their activities and how those activities impact results.

Instructions: (1) List your top five high payoff activities as they relate to Defending & Farming the account. (2) List one to five impediments (obstacles) for each high payoff activity. (3) Brainstorm solutions that can eliminate or reduce the impact of each impediment. (4) Enter action steps on Plan of Action page.

Top Five High Payoff Activities	Impediments (Obstacles)	Possible Solutions
	1.	1.
	2.	2.
1.	3.	3.
	4.	4.
	5.	5.

The next task is completing the Relationship Matrix, what I call the Political Capital Worksheet. I used drop-down menus in a Word document and have illustrated the choices below. There are two matrixes to complete. One is for sphere of influence inside the current sales opportunity and the other is for sphere of influence outside the current sales opportunity. Obviously, whenever possible we want to leverage the influence of people we know within the account, even if they are in a different business unit or geographic location.

Sphere of Influence (Inside Sales Current Opportunity)					
Contact's Name	Title	Value Chain	Relationship	Influence	Relationship Owner's Name
		• Executive • Functional Manager • Line Manager (Supervisor) • Front-Line Employee	• Sponsor • Personal Ally • Neutral (On the Fence) • Favors a Competitor	• High • Moderate • Low	

Answering the following six questions can sometimes be painful, especially to those who have spent many months developing an existing account. The potential answers to the questions are controlled using choices from a drop-down menu.

Questions	Drop-Down Menu Choices
1. Based on the Political Capital worksheet, are you positioned to Defend & Farm this account so you can grow revenue according to plan?	A. Very much so B. Somewhat so C. Not at all
2. How detailed is your knowledge concerning this account's business problems	A. Very detailed B. Somewhat detailed C. Not detailed at all
3. How much do you know about what they measure (Key Performance Indicators)?	A. Very Detailed B. Somewhat Detailed C. Not detailed at all
4. How detailed is your knowledge concerning how the delivery of your solution(s) impacts different business functions within this account?	A. Very detailed B. Somewhat detailed C. Not detailed at all
5. How detailed is your knowledge concerning how the buying and decision-making processes function in this account?	A. Very detailed B. Somewhat detailed C. Not detailed at all
6. Do you and your company have a reputation for solving problems by selling value rather than being a price sensitive vendor on demand?	A. Yes, throughout the organization B. Only with some contacts C. Not at this point in time
7. Do you have access to pursue all sources of potential business across the entire enterprise?	A. Yes, all sources B. Some, but not all sources C. No, only one source at this time

The challenge after answering the questions is establishing what to do next to improve the answers. This is where the Plan of Action and the people named on the very first page come in. Teamwork between members of the client-facing team and Allies and Sponsors within the account pays double dividends. Below is the format I use for a written Plan of Action.

Name of Team Member	Action Step	Target Date	Next Step After Completion

Finally, there is the revenue forecast. This is where the commitment is visualized. Without a forecast, there are no goals, no objectives, nothing to chart. You can set up the forecast using an Excel spreadsheet, or you can create a worksheet in Word.

1. What is your targeted revenue goal for this account?	$	
2. How much revenue do you anticipate from existing business?	$	
3. How much additional business will you need to generate to hit your target? (Subtract #2 from #1)	$	
4. What is your average deal size for the business you win in this account?	$	
5. How many deals will you need to win to hit your Business Development target? (Divide #3 by #4)	#	
6. What do you forecast as your Decision Rate (Closing Rate) in this account? (Divide the total number of proposals sold and lost by the total number of proposals sold.	%	
7. How many proposals must you add to your sales pipeline to hit your new business development target? (Divide #5 by #6)	#	

IMPORTANT FOOTNOTE

Before transitioning from Account Management Practices to New Business Development Practices, I want to describe a real-world picture for all us Doer Sellers who add value to a business enterprise. Consider this a warning, a red flag that hangs from every Doer Seller's wallet. Actually, the red flag also hangs from every salesperson's wallet as well, but it is smaller and not as bright red in color.

Being the best at account management is not enough. You must also master the art of bringing in new client companies. In the real world, this is what inevitably happens to our existing client base.

❖ Our contact Allies and Sponsors retire or get terminated. They get replaced by new contacts who bring in their existing relationships from competing vendors.

❖ The client company gets sold and a new management team replaces the old management team, and what we once delivered is no longer considered a priority.

❖ A business unit or a geographic location that utilized what we delivered gets sold and we immediately lose the source of business.

❖ For good reason, budgets get restricted and are more tightly managed. Suddenly price is driving the decision-making process.

❖ The marketplace changes and what we sold and delivered is no longer required by the current client company. In other words, changes in demand occur suddenly and without warning, and we are unprepared to respond.

The old saying "don't put all your eggs in one basket" is absolutely true. When it comes to sales, there is no argument. If you depend on existing client business only and do not engage in some new business development activity, you will wake up one morning and find yourself dealing with a crisis: a major decline in sales revenue or, worse yet, no sales revenue at all.

For salespeople who are committed to spending all their time selling, this is not a problem. They do a lot of hunting and, depending on their book of business, do a lot less farming. For the Doer Seller, the opposite is true. They do a lot of farming and very little hunting outside of their existing accounts. Take my advice and make a personal commitment to carve out some time to go after new clients. Think about this idea before you read the next section on New Business Development Practices. All clients, no matter how committed, have a relationship life cycle. On the positive side, they end with a natural death with the buyer being totally satisfied. On the negative side, they end with an unnatural death with the buyer being totally dissatisfied. The challenge is in forecasting how long the client will live.

New Business Development Practices

How about an organization that did no new business development! The business just came in the door. Then something happened: the marketplace changed and the phone stopped ringing. In addition, hits on the Web site dropped to what would be considered below minimal. And, of course, everyone blamed marketing. In reality it was a corporate culture issue. The organization was driven by a practitioner culture and needed to change to a sales culture. In other words, it was a Doer culture, not a Sales culture.

After several months of delivering onsite workshops and dedicated one-on-one coaching, the organization adopted a new sales language and thought leadership around using formal sales processes. The Doer Seller model was formalized and tweaked. The full-time salespeople and the Doer Sellers worked together as a team to get results. Identifying new target accounts, making outbound calls, and scheduling first-time sales meetings went from not being a priority to being recognized as a critical business function. Sales from new relationships in new and existing accounts improved. There was a significant improvement in qualifying new prospects, and the Proposal Decision Rate (Closing Rate) improved. The change to a corporate culture where managing a New Business Development Practice was a cultural norm had a major impact on the company's ability to meet and exceed its annual sales quota.

New business development is one of the most challenging subjects for sales leaders, individual sellers, and Doer Sellers. It has always been a struggle and, in challenging economic climates, has become a real "keeps me awake at night" challenge. A lot has been written about how marketing does and does not contribute to the new business development effort. Again, from personal experience as a sales consultant, marketing and sales are frequently out of alignment. Therefore, my focus here is on sales process with suggestions on how to get a better night's sleep.

Understanding Lead Streams

First, let's crystallize our thinking. There are only so many sources of leads, and each category can be rated so that the seller can prioritize his or her investment of time. This is especially important for the Doer Seller. To illustrate, I will use the most commonly used rating system: A, B, C, with an A being the most qualified place to invest your time.

❖ **Inbound (random):**

- ✓ Someone calls you and says he or she was referred to you by someone else. **[A]**

- ✓ You receive an RFP (request for proposal) from a known contact and follow up to qualify the lead. **[A]**

- ✓ You receive a Web and/or telephone inquiry from a known marketing campaign. **[B]**

- ✓ You receive an RFP from an unknown contact and follow up to qualify the lead. **[C]**

- ✓ You receive a Web and/or telephone inquiry from an unknown source. **[C]**

❖ **Outbound (planned):**

- ✓ You ask for and receive a referral from a satisfied client. **[A]**

- ✓ You (the seller) prospect and run an ongoing value marketing campaign. **[A]**

- ✓ You follow up participation from seminars and webinars to generate leads. **[B]**

- ✓ You follow up direct mail marketing campaigns to generate leads. **[B]**

❖ **Networking (planned):**

- ✓ You attend industry events as a presenter and network to generate leads. **[A]**

- ✓ You attend social/community events and network to generate leads. **[B]**

- ✓ You attend industry events as a visitor and network to generate leads. **[C]**

The next most important task from a business development point of view is tracking your effort. Using a Customer Relationship Management System (CRM) is a necessity. The most obvious data to enter is company name and address, contact name and title, phone number, e-mail address, and the lead source. All users of any CRM system struggle with keeping an accurate history. In reality, you cannot know with whom to invest your time unless you track your activity—for example, pre-approach materials sent, calls made, meetings scheduled, meetings held, and proposals and quotes delivered.

New Business Development Strategy and Tactics

There are several sales strategies that sellers use to win business. They can *dominate* the buying process, they can *modify* the buying process, and they can *delay* the buying process. However, for new business development, none is more important than being able to *infiltrate* the buying process. To help clarify what I mean and to make infiltration more doable, I developed a model that defines both strategy and tactics.

Infiltration Strategy

(Breach the Buying Process)

❖ **Use when you want to penetrate an account where the incumbent has a strong position, when you want to divide and conquer over time, or when the prospect is not actively looking for a new vendor.**

✓ Gather business intelligence about specific business issues so you are able to talk about those issues with confidence. Make use of your contacts in companies in the same vertical market, or do research on the Internet.

✓ Gather competitive intelligence from other contacts from within the organization.

❖ **When presenting, demonstrate creative solutions for emerging business challenges.**

✓ Talk about getting some experience with your company so you can demonstrate your true capabilities.

✓ Talk about doing a small piece of the work equal to or better than other vendors.

✓ Talk about reducing the risks associated with using a single vendor.

❖ **When "creating demand" ask questions that uncover need.**

✓ Engage the buyer in *solving an existing problem* that remained unresolved over a period of months or years.

✓ Identify *a need the buyer didn't realize he or she had* and engage the buyer in co-developing a workable solution.

✓ Uncover *the buyer's pain* and creatively relieve the pain without having to move the opportunity to the Service Demand Sales Opportunity practice where there is direct competition.

❖ **When developing business relationships, find the right people.**

✓ The people who govern the buying process and evaluate solution options.

✓ The people who establish the ground rules for buyer/seller interactions and determine the selection criteria as price driven or value driven.

✓ The people who make the final decision based on the short list.

✓ The people who have management authority over a specific business function such as the one you are targeting.

New Business Development Model

Reaching out to new prospects that you never did business with before is a challenging task. This activity goes back to the motivation discussion. When you are in the new business developer role, what is the controlling, motivating factor? The next question is, "do you really have control of which motivator moves you to action?" The answer is yes, you do have control. Your attitude, how you think about the task, is the differentiator. If the process is not clearly defined, then one of the less-desired motivators could become dominant, like fear of rejection. Below is the new business development process I recommend. If a step is not working to your satisfaction, tweak the step. Use power motivation; be in control of the process. For best results, I recommend your new business development effort be vertical-market driven.

1) **Prepare:**

    a. Prepare a sales presentation using software like PowerPoint. A deck of five to seven slides is good; no more than ten is recommended. Use the deck as a conversation guide during the first meeting. The deck should include one slide with relevant issues to a targeted vertical market. If you are running a telephone meeting, I recommend you save the deck as a PDF file and send it to the contact the day before your meeting. The goal of using the PowerPoint deck is to get the prospect to talk so you can discover the pain points, which helps you know how to make the sale.

    b. Prepare two or three different business-value-centric, pre-approach e-mail messages. You will need to run tests on each version to see which gets the best result.

2) **Find Prospects:**

    a. Prospect for accounts that you know for sure use your type of offerings on a regular basis. Create a Chase List.

I recommend you always maintain a list of twenty to thirty live targets that are not in your formal CRM pipeline.

b. Complete research for each selected account to gain insight into its current business conditions. Go to each Web site. You can also go to Yahoo Finance (http://finance.yahoo.com) and do a search to get information.

c. Identify primary contact titles for the A and/or B people. You can obtain this information from the target company's Web site, or you can call reception or the CEO's office. You can also buy business information using Hoovers or OneSource.

i) Note: The A people *govern the resources* that relate to an opportunity, assess problems, and define the metrics that relate to the problem and its solution. The B people *govern the buying process*, evaluate solution options, and establish ground rules for seller/buyer interaction. The C people *govern the proposal process*, select vendors, and negotiate price and delivery options.

d. If you are calling high in the value chain, there is probably an administrative assistant (AA). Obtain that person's contact information. Never ignore the AA; make that person your Ally. He or she is the gatekeeper, and you will not get to the target unless the gatekeeper gives you the "okay to proceed" signal.

3) Make Contact:

a. Make the first call. Leave a voice-mail message that you will be sending an e-mail and that you will put your name in the subject line (for example, *Message from Howard Dion*).

b. If the target contact has an administrative assistant, call that person first. Ask for his/her help in delivering your message or request that they alert the targeted contact about the message you will be sending.

c. Immediately thereafter, send the e-mail. Do not attach any files to the e-mail.

4) **Reply to a *Positive Response* within forty-eight hours.**

a. Follow up by phone to schedule the sales meeting. The meeting can be by telephone or face-to-face, depending on travel time. Face-to-face is always preferred over a telephone meeting. Be persistent and keep calling until you connect with the contact.

b. Schedule the sales meeting and confirm by e-mail. Using an Outlook invite is the preferred method.

c. After your sales presentation, agree to a next step as outlined on the last slide of the PowerPoint deck you sent.

d. Send a letter of understanding via e-mail outlining the agreed-to next steps and follow up for a response in a timely fashion.

5) **Manage a *Negative Response or No Response.***

a. At this juncture you have three choices.

i) Try to make contact anyway and follow up by phone three times within seven business days.

ii) Try another contact in the same company and start with step #2 above.

iii) Push out forty-five to sixty days and start the outreach process over from scratch. The majority of the time, the target will not remember your first attempt.

| Identify the Right Contact in a Target Account | Make a Call to Alert the Contact about the E-mail | Send a Pre-approach E-mail | Follow up and Schedule the First Sales Meeting |

Everything discussed about new business development on the previous pages was constructed around a traditional way of thinking. And yes, that thinking has a lot of value and still works. But today, we live in the world of technology, and I would be remiss if I did not mention social networking.

Social networking is a communication system, and it obviously has value from a sales and marketing perspective. There are actually hundreds of social networking sites, but only a few have gained significance from a business perspective. The most commonly recognized names—Facebook, Twitter, Myspace, and LinkedIn—are great places to advertise. Using social networking is a business function—an advertising medium just like newspapers used to be before the Internet started to dominate our world. From an individual business developer perspective, online conversations are dangerously time consuming, and perhaps even distracting. With that said, social networking sites are a great place to meet people and get personal introductions to people high in the value chain. But after that, it is back to the traditional way of thinking. As of today, *nothing has replaced the phone call and the face-to-face sales meeting.*

In closing this discussion, I recommend that you write your own activity-driven *Weekly Business Development Plan of Action*. Monitor your results against the plan at the end of every week. If it is not working, change the plan. Below is a simple outline to help get you started. As a footnote, I use the term "existing" accounts below for a reason. Meeting new people in an existing account in a new business unit or geographic location is also considered new business development.

1. How many *new target accounts* do you want to identify to add to your database?

2. How many pre-approach messages will you send to new and existing contacts?

3. How many first-time calls will you make to new and existing contacts?

4. How many sales meetings will you schedule?

5. How many sales meetings will you actually complete?

6. How many quotes will you send?

THE STATS GAME

This is the single most important and self-disciplined activity that any seller can undertake. When I first began Matrix Consulting Group, I tracked my activity and results on a daily basis. In the beginning, I was a Seller Doer and needed an objective way to evaluate my own performance as well as a method to motivate myself. Goal setting was my answer. I created a scorecard that was driven by two criteria: points earned and the weekly goals established to earn the points. I made working on new business development a game.

One day a client asked me how I managed to keep myself going working alone out of my house. At the time, I did not know that he was thinking of leaving his VP of sales position so that he could go out on his own as a consultant. What happened next was a profitable experience for both of us. He paid me to deliver the Point System concept to his sales team. The first version of the Point System indentified specific activities, and each activity was assigned a point value. These were then tracked on a weekly basis against a monthly Plan of Action. The monthly planner page looked like this:

Activity Description	Assigned Points	Monthly Goal	Points Earned
Number of new target accounts identified to pursue	2		
Number researched on the Internet	3		
Number entered in database with complete contact information	3		
Number of calls made prior to sending pre-approach message	2		
Number of pre-approach value messages sent to target contacts	5		

Activity Description	Assigned Points	Monthly Goal	Points Earned
Number of calls made to follow up pre-approach messages	7		
Number of other calls made to develop business	5		
Number of sales meetings scheduled	7		
Number of sales meetings actually held	7		
Number of technical/content management meetings held	7		
Number of quotes/proposals delivered	7		
Number of sales closed and won	5		
Number of referrals obtained	2		
		Monthly Total	

In 2009, I started to work with a client that had a negative reaction to the Point System. He wanted the tracking but felt assigning points to each activity was a meaningless time killer. To meet that client's need, I redesigned the scorecard. There were two versions, one for salespeople and Doer Sellers and one for telephone prospectors.

Again, when I first started the business, I had no recurring revenue streams. Therefore, I was fulfilling a Seller Doer role rather than the Doer Seller role. I had to make a sale before I could deliver what I sold. What I found most helpful, from a performance improvement point of view, was the end result tracking that was calculated as a year-to-date number. Over the last ten years, what I track has evolved and changed based on my experiences in working with clients. I now recommend these five metrics to every client who requests one-on-one sales coaching with the objective of improving sales performance.

1. The Percentage of Time Actually Spent on Sales

2. Calls to Meetings Conversion Rate

3. Meeting to Proposal Conversion Rate

4. Decision Rate

5. Average Deal Size Won and Average Deal Size Lost

Recently, a client asked me how keeping track of these stats would help his direct sales reports. He was very concerned about the lack of results of one of his new hires. My answer was as follows. First, we can compare results between different sellers and look for exceptions that are either significantly higher or lower. Then we can start asking questions to identify the strength or weakness. Keep in mind that the individual using the scorecard is constantly aware of his or her own performance on a daily basis. In essence, the scorecard is a mechanism for self-management. Finally, and most important, the scorecard acts as a platform for goal setting. My client nodded his head in agreement and encouraged his people to use the scorecard.

The scorecard is not intended to act as a cure for poor performance. It is however, a tool that gives the user insight into their own behavior in the form of activities and results. The tool is an Excel spreadsheet with weekly tabs and a final monthly recap tab. The illustration on the next page shows the new version.

Here is another story that reflects the impact of the scorecard concept. I have not worked with this client for over three years, yet I still get copied on the scorecard that the director of marketing and business development sends to his boss on a weekly basis. I still make comments based on the data, sometimes positive and sometimes not so positive, just like I did when I was under contract. My reasoning is this: I delivered the scorecard concept and asked the client to be disciplined and diligent in tracking and reporting the sales stats. My weekly comments empower the user of the process and help maintain the discipline within the organization. Spending ten minutes of my time each week keeps me connected and committed to what I value most, the relationship.

New Version of the Scorecard

Results	Week 1	Week 2	Week 3	Week 4	Actual Results	Goals	% of Goal
Number of Sales Closed	1	0	4	0	5	8	63%
Required Activities	**Week 1**	**Week 2**	**Week 3**	**Week 4**	**Actual Results**	**Goals**	**% of Goal**
Number of Quotes/Proposals Delivered	3	4	2	0	9	16	56%
Number of Meetings Completed (Phone or Face-to-Face)	6	7	12	0	25	48	52%
Number of Meetings Scheduled	3	3	5	0	11	12	92%
Number of Calls Made to Schedule Meetings	65	59	66	0	190	240	79%
Number of Marketing E-mails Sent	45	41	51	0	137	180	76%
Performance Metrics	**Week 1**	**Week 2**	**Week 3**	**Week 4**	**Actual Results**	**Goals**	**% of Goal**
Decision Rate	33%	0%	200%	0%	56%	65%	86%
Meeting to Proposal Conversion Rate	50%	57%	17%	0%	36%	50%	72%
Calls to Meetings Conversion Rate	5%	5%	8%	0%	6%	20%	30%

Note: The actual results come from the seller's personal tracking data and/or from a corporate CRM system.

STRATEGIC SELLING PRACTICES

Here is a simple definition of Strategic Selling Practices: the process used to differentiate strategic sales opportunities from transactional sales opportunities and the process used to pursue and win strategic sales opportunities while making effective use of the seller's time. The key phrase is "making effective use of the seller's time." The major sales effectiveness companies competing for business all strive to achieve this objective. However, some do that job better than others.

Besides the model illustrated earlier in this book, there is another methodology used to quickly differentiate between a strategic sales opportunity and a transactional sales opportunity. It involves developing a series of questions that are used by every seller in the organization to objectively help make the decision. Below is an example of the questions that I use with my clients.

The questions simply get a "yes" or "no" answer. Each "yes" answer is equal to ten points. If the seller does not know the answer, he or she must ask questions and get the answers from the buyer. Not being able to get the answers says a lot about the nature of the sales opportunity. There is a high probability that the opportunity is strategic when it earns fifty-plus points.

1. Is face-to-face contact expected and/or required by the buyer, and can it be financially justified?

2. Was the opportunity discovered early in the sales cycle?

3. Does the opportunity have an extended sales cycle timeline (greater than three months)?

4. Does the opportunity fit nicely within one of our core business offerings?

5. Do you have a moderate to high probability of meeting with the people who own the project?

6. Do you have a moderate to high probability of meeting with the people who own the problem linked to the project?

7. Do you have a moderate to high probability of meeting with the people who own the strategy linked to solving the problem?

8. Is the dollar value of this opportunity higher than your year-to-date (YTD) average deal size won?

9. Has the client encouraged the incumbent and other vendors to bid on this opportunity?

10. There are no "ground rules" that control or prohibit seller-to-buyer interaction?

Keep in mind that in smaller companies, people sometimes wear more than one hat. One contact may own the project, the problem associated with the project, and the strategy that is driving the need to solve the problem.

So what is the process used to pursue and win strategic sales opportunities? Strategy is the framework which guides the nature and direction of a sales campaign, and tactics are the action steps that accomplish the seller's strategy. In order for a sales strategy to be effective, it must encompass the following components:

1) A specific sales objective defined as (a) what you are selling (the product and/or service), (b) to whom, (c) for how much in dollars, and (d) by when.

2) A knowledge audit that identifies missing information around key areas, such as the business quality of the

opportunity, value vs. price, internal politics, and competitive intelligence.

3) A Plan of Action (tactics) to obtain the answers to the unanswered questions.

4) A relationship audit that allows for analysis of the seller's contacts to determine if the contact is an Ally, supports a competitor, or sits on the fence and is neutral.

5) An influence audit that allows for analysis of the seller's contacts to determine the level of influence the seller has on the final buying decision.

6) A methodology to build a political capital worksheet based on the results of the relationship and influence audits so that tactics can be defined and implemented.

7) Definitions of competitive tactics and counter-tactics and a Plan of Action (tactics) on how to utilize the tactics during the current sales campaign.

In the final analysis, we are asking the seller to stop and think about his or her behavior, what he or she says and does to win the business. Under this scenario, winning is not about instinct or product knowledge or personal experience. It's about careful planning and thoughtful execution of the plan. It is about consistency, about tweaking the process to improve results, and about thinking before we engage the competition in the field of battle.

Before I move on to discussing Sales Opportunity Practices, I would like to make this recommendation. The sales leader must mandate absolute compliance to the standards around each of the Sales Management Practices. Each practice must be carefully defined and communicated. The same is true for the Doer Seller. The difference can be twofold depending on the size of the organization. If it is large, with many Doer Sellers, then senior management must take on the role and define expectations. If the organization is small, then each Doer Seller must individually take on the role and wear three hats: the Doer hat, the Seller hat, and the Sales Leader hat.

To clearly define the role, I recommend a job description that answers these questions:

- ❖ **Accountability:**
  - ➢ What business functions do you own? What are you liable for to your employer?

- ❖ **Responsibility:**
  - ➢ What is the proper sphere or extent of your activities within each area of accountability?

- ❖ **Authority to Act:**
  - ➢ Concerning your areas of accountability, when must you seek approval from your manager before taking action?

- ❖ **Measurement Criteria:**
  - ➢ What will you measure in order to manage your responsibilities?

- ❖ **Reporting Criteria:**
  - ➢ What reports are required by a specific deadline? What information must be maintained? What technologies are required in the position?

- ❖ **Qualifications:**
  - ➢ What personal attributes are you required to exhibit and what competencies are you required to perform in this position?

CHAPTER 3—SALES OPPORTUNITY PRACTICES

Sales Opportunity Practices are owned by the salesperson and the Doer Seller equally. Management can, and should, interact in these practices, but only as Task Master, Problem Solver, Coach, or Mentor. In my job at Matrix Consulting Group, I acted as a Coach 80% of the time and was split between Problem Solver and Mentor 20% of the time. Obviously, management style is also a critical factor. With that said, I suggest that a manager must play different roles with different people depending on the circumstances. Below is a model that I use to help people visualize in more concrete terms what I mean by having the flexibility to play different roles when managing salespeople.

Manager's Role	The Task Master	The Problem Solver	The Coach	The Mentor
Use When	Performance Is Below Expectation	The Seller Asks for Help or Requires Help Based on Observation	Performance Is at Expectation and Has the Potential to Exceed Expectation	Performance is Consistently Above Expectation
Manager's Focus	On Seller's Job Description and Formal Sales Processes	On the Current Task Scenario or Specific Sales Challenge	On Utilization of Adopted Formal Sales Processes	On the Individual's Personal and/ or Professional Needs
Manager's Behavior	Hierarchical and Impersonal	Prescriptive and Advisory	Insightful, Challenging, and Collaborative	Nurturing and Respectful

Manager's Role	The Task Master	The Problem Solver	The Coach	The Mentor
Expected Seller's Response	Compliance to New Defined Expectation	Acceptance and Implementation of Recommendations	Personal Initiative in Utilization of the Recommendations	Personal Initiative to Get Involved in the Relationship
Intended Outcome	Restore Acceptable Performance Levels	Improve Current Task Scenario or Overcome Specific Sales Challenge	Improve Core Sales Competencies	Personal and/ or Professional Growth
Timing of Interaction	Weekly One-on-One Meetings	Pipeline Meetings and One-on-One Meetings on a Weekly Basis	Pipeline Meetings and One-on-One Meetings on a Weekly Basis	Monthly or Bi-Monthly One-on-One Meetings

This model is a guide to illustrate the potential leadership differences that can have a positive impact on overall performance. Connected to this model are the four Sales Opportunity Practices: Satisfy Demand, Service Demand, Create Demand, and Defend & Farm. Each practice has its own unique demands, set of circumstances, and associated sales processes that require a specific skill set and mental and emotional discipline. The majority of my Sales Insight Tools and Sales Planners support these practices and work best in the Problem Solving or Coaching Roles.

I have always believed that adopting a common sales language is critically important. A common sales language speeds communications. Having meaningful content backing up the words that are used is even more important. In the world of technology, that is how one application is able to talk to another application and get the job done. Think about the technical communication challenges between Microsoft and Apple applications. It is impressive when you sit in on a sales meeting and people talk back and forth using the same language. Better yet is when full-time professional salespeople and Doer Sellers talk the same sales language. In an organization that has different business practices, those practitioners that manage and work in those practices speak their own language. Therefore, having a common sales language that links the practices from a communication perspective has a major impact on overall productivity. When that happens, cross-selling becomes much easier and much more of an accepted norm.

Satisfy Demand

Satisfying Demand occurs when a buyer continues to purchase a product and/or service from the seller as the preferred vendor. At first glance, you would think that satisfying demand is a simple process that requires little effort. In fact, renewals do take a certain amount of work from the delivery team in making sure the client continues to be "satisfied" with what is being delivered. There are several different sales scenarios that come into play to Satisfy Demand.

1. No salesperson owns the account. The account is often called a house account. The delivery team or practitioners have no sales accountability other than providing ongoing delivery and/or customer service and support.

2. A salesperson owns the account and only makes personal contact when the client becomes dissatisfied with what is being delivered or decides they no longer need what the seller has to offer.

3. A Doer Seller owns the account and manages the revenue stream.

In many organizations, especially in the technology and financial services sectors, there could be hundreds of accounts that are characterized as Satisfy Demand accounts. That is why the above three sales scenarios always carry a *red flag*. The danger is in ignoring or missing out on other sales opportunities. It is impossible for a seller to spend time on hundreds of Satisfy Demand accounts and also be successful at Key Account management and/or new business development. Therefore, we need to refer back to Account Management Practices to better capitalize on the revenue potential of these accounts. When companies have an unmanageable number of these accounts, they could be missing incredible opportunities for organic growth. Every Satisfy Demand account should be classified as Key, Secondary, or Tertiary.

Satisfy Demand buyers have these characteristics:

* They view what they are buying as a product or service commodity.

* They focus on options and solutions to specific ongoing business challenges.

* They are motivated by having a quick fix or by an ongoing business initiative.

* The need is clearly defined and accepted by senior management.

* The sense of urgency is immediate and recurring.

* The sales timeline is short-term, usually quarterly or annual.

* Funding is preapproved.

Service Demand

Servicing Demand occurs when:

1. The buyer is looking for a solution to a problem, has no relationship with an incumbent, and encourages many vendors to bid on the business; or

2. The buyer is looking for a solution to a problem, has a working relationship with an incumbent, but decides to replace the incumbent because they are dissatisfied; or

3. The buyer is looking for a solution to a problem, is forced by a mandate to get competitive bids, and may want to leverage the bids to get a lower price from an incumbent.

Servicing Demand clearly means the buyer knows what he or she is looking to buy and there is always competition. This is an area where the majority of Doer Sellers and professional salespeople spend most of their time.

Servicing Demand is also the primary driver of complex sales opportunities where strategic selling strategy and tactics become critical. Again, look at the source of the lead. Inbound leads have a high probability of being Servicing Demand. Outbound leads have a lower probability of being characterized as Servicing Demand. However, there is one fact that always surfaces when a seller is developing business from his or her own outbound lead effort. They often uncover Service Demand sales opportunities that they would have missed had they not made that *cold call* to a prospective client.

Service Demand is where I place the majority of Requests for Proposals (RFPs) and Requests for Quotes (RFQs), and it does not matter whether you know the originator of the RFP or RFQ or not. Therefore, qualifying the opportunity very early in the sales cycle is the number one priority. You must be able to quickly decide whether or not the opportunity is worth pursuing. You could spend hours chasing an opportunity that you can never win. Unfortunately, this happens all too often. We have meetings, use corporate resources to write the proposal, and add the opportunity to the sales pipeline all at the expense of opportunities that we have a more realistic chance of winning.

At this point, I would like to influence your thinking. Review these questions and use your answers as a guide to help make that critical *"pursue"* or *"no pursue"* decision.

❖ Are there are any rules of play that would prevent you from making ongoing contact with people in the buyer's organization?

❖ From the buyer's perspective, can you validate that your industry and/or project delivery experience is equal to or better than that of other competing vendors?

❖ Do you, or does someone else in your company, have a personal relationship with other contacts in the buyer's organization whose sphere of influence is outside of the current sales opportunity? If the answer is yes, can you capitalize on those relationships to help with the current opportunity?

❖ Are there any technical, geographic, or timeframe challenges associated with delivering the requested solution that would negatively impact the final buying decision?

❖ Are you able to obtain information about the buyer's budget restrictions before you submit the final proposal?

❖ Will your company have to lower its fees in order to be competitive so you can close the sale?

❖ Are you able to gather competitive intelligence so you can employ competitive counter-tactics that will help you close the sale?

I would like to be able to tell one great story about Servicing Demand that would illustrate the concept, but I cannot. The challenge is that all of the clients I worked with spent the majority of their selling time competing for business. The pipelines were filled with opportunities from existing clients who wanted competitive bids; or from inbound leads driven by a successful marketing effort; or from cold calls that uncovered an existing need. Many of the opportunities were strategic in nature, and many more were transactional. For me, an uncomfortable number of sales opportunities found a home in the seller's pipeline and sat there for months and months. In many instances, it was a battle to get the seller to mark the opportunity as lost.

There is one very important takeaway from this experience. Prospects will have a seller spend his or her corporate resources to deliver a proposal and never make a buying decision. Prospects will have a seller spend his or her corporate resources to deliver a proposal and never get the required funding. With all that said, a large percentage of every company's annual revenue comes from winning Service Demand sales opportunities. Servicing Demand is hard work. It is time-consuming, expensive, and rewarding all at the same time. When you Service Demand, the buyer is in control. When you Create Demand, you, the seller, are in control. This difference is why my personal Sales Opportunity Practice preference is to Create Demand for my products and services.

Create Demand

Creating Demand for your product or service is about opening doors. It is the essence of new business development and encompasses three important skill sets:

1. Being able to engage a buyer in solving an existing problem that remained unresolved over a period of months or years.

2. Being able to identify a need the buyer didn't realize they had and being able to engage the buyer in co-developing a solution.

3. Being able to uncover the buyer's pain and being able demonstrate how you can relieve, reduce, or eliminate the pain using your company's offerings.

Sounds like something every Doer Seller and every professional salesperson should be able to master with some training, and perhaps some time and experience. In reality, Creating Demand is the single most challenging task in the process of new business development. Over the last ten years, this is where I spent the majority of my sales training time and where I made the most significant impact. To my surprise, many sales leaders and sellers were just not familiar with the term "Create Demand."

Creating Demand starts with who the seller targets when trying to get in the door. The higher in the value chain, the better. From personal experience, I can tell you entering the sales cycle below the functional manager level will generate minimal Create Demand sales success.

- *The Executive:* Generally a person responsible for running an organization, although the exact nature of the role varies depending on the organization. In general terms, these individuals own the strategy.

- *The Functional Manager:* A person who has management authority over a specific business function, such as sales or market research. Functional managers have ongoing responsibilities, including ensuring that goals and objectives are aligned with the organization's overall strategy and vision. These individuals usually own the problem.

- *The Line Manager:* A business term to describe the administration of activities that contribute directly to the output of products or services. In a corporate hierarchy, a "line manager" holds authority in a vertical "line" (chain of command) and/or over a particular product line. He or she is charged with meeting corporate objectives in a specific functional area or line of business. A line manager is sometimes titled as a supervisor. These individuals usually own the project.

- *The Front-Line Employee:* These individuals are responsible to complete a specific job based on a job description and usually report up the value chain to a line manager or supervisor.

The next thing to consider is a learned behavior, a traditional way of thinking about a potential client's political power grid. This thinking impacts behavior and is, for the most part, subconscious on the part of the seller. The seller sits in the middle of the potential client organization and strives to develop relationships with people in one or more of the functions illustrated in this model.

Now expand your thinking around this model. Within each of these business functions are people at different levels of the value chain. Titles aside, the objective is to develop and implement a political strategy: a conscious effort to develop personal relationships with the "right people." I suggest that we strive to label each relationship with one of these unofficial Seller Titles.

- ❖ **Personal Ally**

- ❖ **Sponsor**

- ❖ **Primary Sponsor**

I will define these titles in more detail in the section titled "Forget about Titles" on page 85.

My largest Create Demand sale happened like this. I made a cold call and got a meeting with the acting vice president of sales. During the presentation, I discovered a corporate culture problem that had never been addressed. It was a problem that was preventing the organization from growing. The acting vice president of sales became my Ally and Sponsor and scheduled a meeting for me with the CEO, a meeting which the acting vice president of sales also attended. The CEO became my Primary Sponsor and scheduled a meeting with me and the chairman of the board to explain the use of the unbudgeted expense for my services. This experience crystallized my thinking around the Create Demand Sales Opportunity Practice.

Defend & Farm

Here is a simple definition of "Defend & Farm": when the account management team defends the account from competitive encroachment and continues to expand their reach within the account to grow profitable revenue streams in other business units and geographic locations, and when the account management team is able to generate revenue from other products and services not previously delivered within the account.

I have seen account management teams consisting of ten people and account management teams consisting of one person. If the client is a very large corporation with billions in revenue and the selling organization has really penetrated the account, there could be many sellers assigned to different geographic locations or business units. Of course, if the selling organization is small and the client is a billion-dollar company spread all over the world, there is major challenge associated with Defending & Farming the account.

What happens when a Doer Seller delivers his or her services in several large accounts and is expected to grow revenue in each of those accounts? Things get really complicated when there is also a salesperson assigned to an account. The only manageable answer is teamwork and planning. Using an organized sales process as a team, such as a Key Account Plan or Strategic Ownership Account Plan, drives a goal-driven strategy that can achieve results in a timely manner. Not planning, not working together as a team with shared goals and objectives, does not achieve the best results.

I recommend the adoption of a set of team values that everyone on the team signs off on, and I do mean in writing. To clarify, a team includes the people who sell for a living, the people who write the proposals, and the people who deliver the product and/or service. Below is an example of what I mean by a set of values:

- ❖ We openly share what we learn about projects, people, and practices (what works and what doesn't).

- ❖ We proactively communicate information that is of value to other team members.

- ❖ We strive to set and keep individual commitments to our sales activity goals.

❖ We strive to maintain client satisfaction.

❖ We focus on increasing repeat and referral business.

❖ We develop and deliver quality deliverables that can be referenced to other prospects within the account.

❖ We leverage our company's portfolio of skills and capabilities.

❖ We are 100% committed to Defend & Farm the account as a team.

I was running a monthly meeting with the sales staff of a small technology company and decided to introduce the idea of using an Upfront Contract. An Upfront Contract is a document that everyone on the team signs and, by doing so, makes a personal commitment to honor and abide by. My reasoning in this case was that everyone on the team was doing his or her own thing. This behavior, in some cases, was causing internal conflicts between the sales team, the Doers, and the two very productive Doer Sellers. The conflicts were inhibiting sales results. Part of the content said this:

The undersigned agrees to abide by the following affirming behaviors:

1. Shares openly and authentically with others regarding personal feelings, opinions, thoughts, and perceptions about problems that are both internal and external to the organization.

2. Acts as a team player who works cooperatively with others.

3. Takes personal ownership of problems, does not blame others, and offers potential creative solutions.

4. Demonstrates confidence in the company's delivery capabilities.

5. Demonstrates pride in the company and what the company seeks in return for the business value it offers to clients.

6. Demonstrates a personal commitment in meeting the needs of each internal customer and external customer.

7. Demonstrates that the client's needs come before the individual employee's needs.

8. Demonstrates integrity and ethical behavior when working with others.

9. Openly shares knowledge about projects, people, and practices in terms of what works and what doesn't work.

10. Sets and then works hard to achieve personal performance improvement goals.

11. Agrees to abide by the use of any and all sales processes, to include sales methodologies, Sales Planners, and Insight Tools.

12. Gives permission to any other team member to call the undersigned on his/her behavior when that behavior is in conflict with the above affirming behaviors.

I explained the idea and then gave each person a copy of the Upfront Contract. We reviewed the content line item by line item. There was some discussion about wording, and we did make some edits. Then came the moment of truth! I asked everyone to sign the document and pass the signed copy to me for safekeeping. Then someone asked a question. "How will we know if someone does not abide by the rules?" "Good question," I said. "You all work together as a team and no one operates in a vacuum. You will see the behavior and can take the person aside and confront the issue, or you can bring it up at one of our monthly meetings." There was some further discussion, and we agreed that we would only confront someone from behind the scenes and never in a public setting at a team meeting. Everyone signed the document except for one person who wanted a day to think about the content. The peer pressure was immediate, and the person reluctantly signed the document.

Over the coming weeks there was some behavioral improvement, and some of the conflicts diminished in intensity. I learned from this experience and in retrospect would do two things differently. First, I would assign one person to manage the Upfront Contract rather than leaving it as a self-governing process. Second, I would print the document, frame it, and hang it over everyone's desk. The old saying "out of sight, out of mind" really carries a lot more weight when you implement an idea like this.

CHAPTER 4—KNOWLEDGE BANK (IMPORTANT SALES IDEAS)

Consider this chapter as a series of mini workshops or seminars. At first glance the subject titles may seem disconnected. In fact, the information is a thread that stitches together the fabric of selling in a competitive sales environment.

SALES MEETINGS

Think about the idea of conducting a sales meeting when you are not a professional full-time salesperson. What do you do? What do you say to the potential client to pique his or her interest? How do you close the sale? If you are a Doer Seller, the process of conducting a successful sales meeting can be disruptive, challenging, and enjoyable all at the same time. A sales meeting is not a *capabilities* presentation where the seller does all the talking about his or her products and services. A sales meeting has a purpose: to uncover the client's needs and get agreement on the next step that brings the selling organization closer to a sale. The flow of a sales meeting should go something like this:

The Concept	The Agenda	Details of the Discussion
The client's current and future circumstances cause client needs, and your product or service features provide benefits that satisfy those needs.	Opening to gain credibility and interest	• The first part of the sales presentation talks about your company's expertise (maybe ten to fifteen minutes) • The way you present gives you personal currency (enthusiasm and passion are key)
	Probe the current conditions in the client's environment	• Ask questions about: ✓ the business environment ✓ how the company utilizes the kinds of products and services you sell ✓ what the company likes and doesn't like about other vendors who sell what you sell ✓ KPIs* & CSFs** (make a list)
	Identify what needs to change to improve the situation	• Identify what is malfunctioning • List the causes of the pain • Prioritize the "pain point" list
	Explain your solution	• Help the client *visualize* your solution • Deliver your *business value* message
	Close on the next step in the sales process	• Clarify how both the formal and informal buying process work • Get agreement as to the next step

* **Key Performance Indicators (KPIs):** measurements of human or organization performance.

** **Critical Success Factors (CSFs):** specific issues considered most vital to the achievement of organizational strategy or the area's most sensitive to the organization's success or failure.

SALES MEETING OUTLINE

1) **Explore Key Performance Indicators and/or Critical Success Factors**

   a. Ask about what they measure that is critical to the organization, business unit, department, or his/her job performance

   b. Ask about current initiatives or projects that are critical to the organization, business unit, department, or his/her job performance

   c. Use your own client examples to help stimulate dialogue

2) **Explore Malfunctions (What's Broken)**

   a. Ask about what kind of things go wrong

   b. Obtain a list of reasons that explain the malfunctions

   c. Prioritize the list from the most painful to least painful

3) **Confirm the Pain**

   a. Feed back what you heard and get agreement

4) **Validate Impact**

   a. Ask for justification of the most painful reasons

   b. Validate the measures

   c. Determine a dollar amount or a number or a percentage that will validate your value proposition in terms of ROI

5) Diagnose Impact

a. Find out who else in the organization is impacted

b. Go up and down the value chain

c. Find out how they are impacted

d. Obtain sponsorship so you can meet these people if appropriate

6) Confirm Prime Buying Motives

a. Feed back what you heard and get agreement

7) Visualize Capabilities

a. Ask if you can try out a few ideas

b. Create different scenarios

c. Try to get the prospect to visualize a solution and to see the ROI

8) Explore Buying Process

a. Discuss the formal buying process

b. Find out who and how

c. Discuss the informal buying process

d. Find out who and how

9) Confirm the Next Step

a. Get agreement on the next step

b. Finalize who, when, and where

DIFFERENTIATING YOURSELF

For some sellers, differentiating themselves from the competition is extremely difficult; for others it is a walk in the park. No matter what vertical market you occupy, no matter how big or small your company, differentiating yourself from the competition is a critical step and has a major impact on winning business. The differentiating process starts during a sales or capability presentation and continues during the delivery process. How this is accomplished has a major impact on account management and how the account management team Defends & Farms an account.

Think about the process as climbing a ladder, only this ladder is made of rungs that are very slippery and the spacing between rungs is far apart. You cannot just step up; you have to reach and pull yourself up with your intellect and emotions in order to get the leverage you need to reach the next step in the differentiation process.

<u>The Most Impact</u>

❖ Rung #5: Seller, practitioner, and buyer interaction *(Top of the Differentiation Ladder)*

  ✓ The seller(s) and the practitioner(s) have developed a solid working relationship with the client contacts and have consistent, ongoing, face-to-face interaction. The relationship encompasses understanding the contact's personal and professional goals. Occurs after the sale is closed and during the delivery process.

❖ Rung #4: Seller and buyer interaction

  ✓ The seller and the client contact start to develop a working relationship that is built on trust.

Requires face-to-face contact. The seller has a basic understanding of the client contact's professional goals and objectives and the business needs of the client contact's employer. Occurs during the sales cycle of Strategic Sales Opportunities (Complex Sales) only.

Level Playing Field between Vendors Chasing the Business

❖ Rung #3: Discussion about product offering and service delivery options

   ✓ Occurs early in the sales cycle during the sales/capabilities presentation process.

❖ Rung #2: Discussion about seller's company history and experience

   ✓ Occurs early in the sales cycle during the sales/capabilities presentation process.

❖ Rung #1: Discussion about price and value *(Bottom of the Differentiation Ladder)*

   ✓ Occurs early in the sales cycle as the seller discovers the buyer's budget restrictions and talks about the seller's company's price-to-value ratio.

SALES CHALLENGES AND A CHANGING BUSINESS PARADIGM

I have worked with many sellers in different verticals with varied levels of sales experience. I sometimes use the term "service organization" and have found that for some, the term is confusing. To eliminate the confusion, here is my definition: a service organization represents a business function, such as...

- Customer Service

- Finance

- Human Resources

- Information Technology

- Market Research

- Marketing

- New Product Development

- Procurement

- Sales

An internal service organization has internal customers and an external service organization has external customers. This distinction is important. If I am selling to an internal service organization, then that organization's internal customer can have a major impact on the buying process. What I call *political influence* usually comes into play, especially with complex sales opportunities where there is more than one decision maker. In my business, I sold to sales organizations that had external customers. The probability of those external customers having any influence on the decision-making process was nonexistent. But suppose I sold to the market research organization whose internal customer was new product development? I enter the buying process directly with the market research decision-making team. However, the VP of new product development has a relative or a friend who sells what I sell and uses his *political influence* to push the business toward that seller rather than to me.

Over the last ten years, changes in the internal service organization's business paradigm have had an indirect impact on external service organizations. However, there has been a direct impact on business-to-business selling organizations. A business paradigm represents how people think and act within a business within a vertical market.

Based on these changes, here is my advice. Do your homework, do the research, know what is happening in those vertical markets that are your primary source of sales revenue. If you want to increase market share, understand the internal service organization's business paradigm and link your sales presentation to that paradigm. Be prepared when you make a capabilities presentation to an internal service organization and its internal customers. Below is the paradigm model that you can use to help your thinking. You should work to get answers to these questions.

- ❖ **Employment practices for the enterprise:**
  - ➤ Is staffing based on an organizational chart, or is staffing based on the work that needs to be done?

- ❖ **Business drivers for the enterprise:**
  - ➤ Is there an external focus based on speed-to-market to gain competitive advantage, or is there an external focus based on business process improvement?

- ❖ **Business trends driving the enterprise:**
  - ➤ Is it about emerging technologies, or is it about linking to the global economy?

❖ **The Internet:**

  ➢ Is it used for marketing and branding strategies, or is it used as a distribution channel? Or, perhaps both?

❖ **How buying decisions are made:**

  ➢ Are they based on who has the right resources with the right expertise, or are they based on who has the right expertise to offer the right solutions at the right price?

❖ **How Internal Service Organization budgets are managed by the enterprise:**

  ➢ Are they indirect and institutional in nature (KPIs and benchmarks are not required to justify funding) or direct allocated by how resources are shared across the enterprise (KPIs and benchmarks are required to justify funding)?

❖ **How Internal Service Organizations market themselves:**

  ➢ Are they reactive, offering known quality solutions to meet current needs, or are they proactive, selling creative solutions for emerging challenges?

❖ **How Internal Service Organizations manage business strategy:**

  ➢ Is the organization independent of the overall business strategy, or is the organization lockstep with the overall corporate business strategy?

Anyone who has been in sales for the last ten years knows that the challenges have intensified and require a more thoughtful go-to-market strategy. If you only have two or three years of sales experience or are a newcomer, the challenge is much more difficult.

I believe the old saying that "knowledge is power" applies here and may be able to help sellers overcome the challenges simply by knowing what they are. Use this list of challenges as a guide. Plan your go-to-market strategy with these challenges in mind.

- ❖ **Challenge #1: Scheduling meetings with executives and functional managers**

  - ➢ There are less people doing more work and time management has become a critical issue

- ❖ **Challenge #2: Getting funding for a project**

  - ➢ Budgets are restricted and very tightly controlled.

  - ➢ Internal business process improvement projects are consuming organizational resources.

- ❖ **Challenge #3: Developing Allies who influence the buying process**

  - ➢ Buyers tend to favor vertical market subject matter experts.

  - ➢ Sellers must be knowledgeable of the overall business strategy in order to demonstrate they have influence (critical).

  - ➢ Senior managers are more focused on their stature within the organization, making them more cautious when developing new relationships.

- ❖ **Challenge #4: Developing Allies who influence the decision process**

  - ➢ Decisions favor those that can demonstrate they have the right expertise (competencies) and the right solution at the right price.

> ➤ Employee performance appraisals, rewards, and recognition are more closely tied to Key Performance Indicators.

> ➤ People at all levels of the value chain are more focused on protecting their own turf.

> ➤ Managers may desire to block or eliminate outside suppliers from delivering services because they fear their company may outsource their business function.

> ➤ Political agendas are more complex and extend up and down the value chain.

❖ **Challenge #5: New business development is more dependent on finding Sponsors who...**

> ➤ Have the ability to take you anywhere in the value chain (up or down) so you can make the sale.

> ➤ Are willing to take the risk associated with personal introductions.

> ➤ Are willing to work behind the scenes to get others to support your ideas so you can make the sale.

> ➤ Have the political capital to influence both the buying process and decision-making process and are willing to spend that capital on your behalf.

> ➤ Can get access to unbudgeted resources (money, people, and time).

❖ **Challenge #6: The seller's commitment to change**

> ➤ Scheduling time to identify target accounts.

> ➤ Scheduling time to maintain a database.

➤ Scheduling time to do research.

➤ Having enough self-discipline and tenacity to follow a process.

➤ Taking personal responsibility to develop the right core sales competencies, such as:

- Business acumen

- Effective verbal and written communication skills (critical)

- Political adeptness

- Relationship management

❖ **Challenge #7: Getting the organization's support when it comes to team selling**

➤ A requirement for less-experienced business developers.

❖ **Challenge #8: The loss of existing relationships**

➤ Changing jobs has become the norm rather than the exception.

- Job dissatisfaction forces change.

- Reorganization forces change.

- A competitive business environment forces change.

➤ On the negative side:

- New hires sometimes offer favored vendor status to their "old job" relationships.

- You lose influence and your inside track to business.

➢ On the positive side:

  - The shoe could be on the other foot and you could be the "old job" relationship.

  - Turnover can be a blessing in disguise and offer new sales opportunities if the old contact was an obstacle.

  - Job instability is a logical reason to develop Allies higher in the value chain.

  - Position yourself today to leverage tomorrow's relationships.

Forget about Titles

For my entire career, I talked about being high in the value chain, especially when working on new business development. Targeting an executive or a functional manager is important, but there is another aspect to the thinking: the buying process from a human perspective. What a person actually does for a living is more important than their title. The individual's management style also plays an important role and can only be discovered through face-to-face contact. Knowing whether your contact uses a dictatorial or participative management style can have a real impact on your sales strategy.

"A" people identify problems relating to their business function, manage the metrics linked to the problems, and govern the resources associated with solving the problems. The "A" people delegate accountability, responsibility, and authority to act to the "B" people.

"B" people govern the buying process, evaluate solution options, establish ground rules for buyer/seller interactions, determine the selection criteria as price driven or value driven, and make the final decision based on the short list. The "B" people delegate accountability, responsibility, and authority to act to the "C" people.

"C" people govern the proposal process, select vendors, send out the RFP, review the proposals, negotiate delivery and pricing options, and create the short list. The "C" people conduct a "bake-off" using the criteria set by the "B" people and line up the vendors to compete for the business.

Now let's look at the three buying zones and how those zones relate to what people actually do for a living.

1. **Seller's Trusted Partner Zone:** The "A" people who identify problems relating to their business functions, manage the metrics linked to the problems, and govern the resources associated with addressing the problems *buy based on their perception of your business value.*

2. **Seller's Problem Solver Zone:** The "B" people who govern the buying process evaluate solution options, establish ground rules for buyer/seller interactions, determine the selection criteria as price driven or value driven, and make the final decision based on the short list *buy based on their perception of the value of your deliverables.*

3. **Seller's Commodity Zone:** The "C" people who govern the proposal process select vendors, send out the RFP, review the proposals, negotiate delivery and pricing options, and create the short list *buy based on your features, functions, and price.*

Linked to this way of thinking are how we as sellers perceive the "A," "B," and "C" people. We have choices.

❖ Choice number one is functional thinking. We can say this contact works in procurement or finance or marketing.

❖ Choice number two is value chain thinking. We can say this contact is an executive or functional manager or line manager.

❖ Choice number three is relationship thinking. We can say this contact is an Ally or Sponsor or Primary Sponsor.

My point is we need to think about all three choices at the same time. Added to the above are two other choices. The contact could support a competitor, or the contact could be neutral and be sitting on the fence. For more clarity on relationship thinking, I offer these definitions.

❖ **Personal Allies** articulate that what you are selling will benefit the organization. They assure you there is a recognized problem that you can solve. They openly communicate accurate information when requested. They also use their influence to support your sales effort.

❖ **Sponsors** demonstrate a willingness to take the risks associated with personal introductions to people higher in the value chain. They demonstrate sponsorship by coordinating the scheduling of meetings with people higher in the value chain. They let you know when they are working behind the scenes to get others to support your ideas.

❖ **Primary Sponsors** are Sponsors who also have one or more of the following characteristics:

➢ Authority to change the rules of the buying process in the middle of the game

➢ Willingness to use that authority on your behalf

> ➤ Political capital to influence the decision-making process

> ➤ Willingness to spend that political capital on your behalf

> ➤ Ability to get access to unbudgeted resources, such as funding

Understanding these labels will also give you insight as to why a competitor has the upper hand, or why a competitor won a piece of business that you thought you had a high probability of winning. Relationship thinking and politics are one and the same. You must develop Allies and Sponsors in Key Accounts in order to successfully Defend & Farm the account.

The Hard-to-Catch Executive

It is true: contacts high in the value chain are hard to catch! From a business development perspective, it is difficult to schedule time at the executive level or with a functional manager if you don't already have a personal relationship. The key is in making contact early in the buying process. Keep in mind:

❖ Executives almost always get involved in the buying process when there is a need to understand current business issues, establish initial project objectives, or set overall project strategy.

❖ Executives sometimes get involved to explore their options, set criteria for vendor evaluation, or examine alternative solutions.

❖ Executives almost never get involved when planning implementation of the project or when supervising or tracking results.

The highest probability of getting a first-time meeting with an executive is through internal or external referrals. The next best thing is personal contact at an off-site meeting like a trade show or business card exchange. Getting in the door from a cold start is difficult, but not impossible. There are roadblocks, and there are also tactics that may help overcome the roadblocks.

1) Roadblock: Screening by the administrative assistant.

   a. Potential solutions: Engage the person in the process from the very beginning. Ask the person to hand deliver your value message. Make the person an Ally by asking for his or her help. Always show respect for his or her position. Ask the administrative assistant for the name, contact number, and e-mail address of a trusted advisor you can contact to audit your company for future business value on behalf of the target executive. *Inspect what you expect!*

2) Roadblock: Schedule too tight.

   a. Potential solutions: Ask to schedule a meeting a couple of weeks out and tell the contact you will confirm the meeting a couple of days before. If there is still an objection ask permission to follow-up in forty-five to sixty days. If the contact agrees, send a confirmation via e-mail thanking the contact for his or her time. If the contact is in driving distance, you could also ask for a breakfast or lunch meeting.

3) Roadblock: What your company offers is not currently a priority.

   a. Potential solutions: Use active listening skills to show empathy for the opinion that has been expressed. Ask for a non-selling business resource meeting so you can have influence in the future. *If you never meet face-to-face, you will never get the call when the need does arise.* Speak from a business perspective, not about your product or service bells and whistles. Share business perspectives new to the executive. *Important: know the trends.* Tell executives something they don't already know about their business or industry.

4) Roadblock: Deferral to someone lower in the value chain.

   a. Potential solutions: Ask for a personal introduction via e-mail and permission to report back after contact is made. Follow through with the follow-up even though the results may be negative. Validate that the person is at the next highest appropriate level where your solution can have an impact. Ascertain that he or she fits into the decision-making process. Title aside, is this person truly influential? Does he or she act as a trusted advisor?

ROI THINKING

Return on Investment, or ROI, thinking is a powerful sales tool. Unfortunately, the concept is frequently overlooked. To become an ROI thinker is not as difficult as you may imagine. Consider this assumption: *buyers make buying decisions to gain a benefit, or they make buying decisions to avoid a loss of some kind.*

If the sales opportunity is a Service Demand scenario, ask probing questions around these two areas. In either case, you will uncover important pain points that can be capitalized upon when trying to close the sale.

1. What are the benefits directly attributable to the solution the prospect is looking to purchase?

2. What could be completely eliminated or significantly reduced by delivering the solution the prospect is looking to purchase?

The next step is discovering the Root Drivers that are linked to the current sales opportunity. A Root Driver could be one of the following or a combination of the two. Keep in mind that when a Root Driver malfunctions or does not meet expectations, it causes pain.

❖ Key Performance Indicators (KPIs): Measurements of human or organization performance.

❖ Critical Success Factors (CSFs): Specific issues considered most vital to the achievement of organizational strategy or the areas most sensitive to the organization's success or failure.

The next technique is especially powerful when a seller is in a new business development mode and trying to Create Demand for their product or service. It is based on a series of questions that are facilitated by the seller. In order to be successful, the seller will need to do his or her homework and have firsthand knowledge concerning the economic, industry, sector, or competitive trends that are, or will be in the near future, impacting the target account.

❖ Discuss the business impact caused by the trend (could be positive or negative).

➢ Identify what benefits can be gained and/or what losses can be avoided as each relates to the trends being discussed.

❖ Discuss your recommended solution.

❖ Discuss how using your solution will eliminate the buyer's pain.

❖ Discuss who will benefit from using your solution. Get the details.

❖ Recommend a reasonable start date for implementing your solution.

❖ Discuss the required investment for implementing your solution. At this point in time, we are talking about a ballpark number.

❖ Discuss the expected timeframe for a Return on Investment after implementing your solution.

❖ Discuss what can be measured that is a good indicator of the ROI associated with your solution. Keep in mind that you can select multiple measures and targets.

❖ Describe and come to agreement on what exceeding expectation looks like, and what being below expectation looks like.

You could experiment with putting an ROI PowerPoint slide into your sales presentation. This strategy works especially well during a face-to-face meeting where the buyer has a printed copy to make notes. In this example, I use a sales scenario to illustrate.

Company Name:	Answers
What is the trend or business issue under discussion?	New business development
What is the negative impact caused by the trend or business issue?	Unacceptable revenue growth
Describe the pain caused by the negative impact.	Not enough profit dollars to invest in R&D
What is the recommended solution?	BD Workshop and three months of one-on-one Coaching
Who will benefit from using your solution?	Salespeople, practitioners, and the owners
What's a reasonable start date for implementing your solution?	June 15
What's the required investment for implementing your solution?	$7,500
What's the expected timeframe for ROI after implementation?	90 days
What can be measured that is a good indicator of the ROI associated with this solution?	Dollars from new sales
What does exceeding expectation look like?	20% more sales Q3 of this year than last year
What does below expectation look like?	The same or fewer dollars sold Q3 of this year than last year

Building a Tactical Playbook

Building a Tactical Playbook is a process that requires a group of people to sit down and capture their knowledge and experience and come to agreement on a series of ideas that have a direct impact on an organization's go-to-market strategy.

Over the last ten years, I built Tactical Playbooks for sales organizations that wanted to implement more effective competitive strategies and tactics, and for internal service organizations that wanted to better market themselves to their internal customers.

Building a playbook is an enlightening experience for all concerned and drives thoughtful organizational change. The playbook's value increases when it is continually updated as business conditions evolve and change. There are three modules in the playbook that you could implement yourself:

❖ Module #1—Positioning

➢ Write a positioning statement so all those on the client-facing team agree to how they want to be perceived as a company or business unit. There can and should be different positioning strategies for different vertical markets.

➢ Define affirming and undermining behaviors in writing so that expectations are clear. Managers and employees alike now have a tool to better self-govern their behavior.

➢ The positioning questions that need to be answered are as follows:

  ▪ WHO: Who are you?

  ▪ WHAT: What business are you in?

  ▪ FOR WHOM: What people/markets do you serve?

  ▪ WHAT NEED: What are the special needs of the people/markets you serve?

- AGAINST WHOM: Who are your competitors?

- WHAT IS DIFFERENT: How do you differentiate yourself?

- SO: What are the benefits? What value do you add?

- WHY: What do you seek in return for the value you add?

❖ Module #2—Strategy

➢ Clearly define the organization's competencies to better understand the engine that drives the business. Competencies are a set of required skills and a foundation of knowledge that allow an organization to perform a particular business function. There are two types of competencies, current and emerging. For an organization, core competencies can encompass a set of global skills, qualities (characteristics), and business processes. In a competitive business environment, competencies are the core engine that drives competitive advantage.

- Defining the organization's competencies also empowers the sales team and Doer Sellers to more easily articulate and sell the organization's business value. The most important outcome is an ability to use the competencies to build Competitive Game Plans.

➢ Clearly define the organization's Key Performance Indicators (KPIs) so people can measure and improve their competency performance and so management can set and achieve meaningful benchmarks that align to overall corporate strategy.

> ➤ Complete a matrix that links competencies to KPIs and rate the quality of each competency. Then evaluate and set performance improvement goals on how the competencies impact the KPIs. A competency that is performed at a moderate to weak level can have a negative impact on the achievement of a KPI.

List your most critical KPIs across the top.										Quality Ratings A=Strong B=Moderate C=Weak D=Unknown
No	List your current and emerging competencies in hierarchical order below:									Quality Rating
I.										

> ➤ Write Preliminary Value Propositions so your sales team owns a method that effectively communicates your business value to prospective clients.

❖ Module #3—Tactics

> ➤ Develop talking points to improve communications at all levels of the value chain while empowering the organization's sales staff to develop Allies and Sponsors who will use their influence on behalf of the selling organization.

> ➤ Develop value statements and probing questions so your staff can better sell your business value, test for and obtain competitive intelligence, and determine

which competencies are most critical to which client contacts.

➢ Develop inoculation messages that can be used preemptively to offset misperceptions about your organization and the competitive tactics of aggressive competitors.

Below is the action plan that will help implement the Tactical Playbook:

1. Learn the positioning statement. Test and correct a sales contact's perception at every opportunity. Clear up misperceptions placed in the prospect's mind by competitors.

2. Take control, be consistent, and brand your company based on how you want to be perceived, not how the competitor wants you to be perceived.

3. Use the affirming behaviors as a roadmap to personal and organizational success. Be aware of your behavior and the behavior of others in the organization. Recognize positive behavior and confront negative behavior.

4. Learn to write compelling value propositions. Use the value proposition to differentiate yourself and your company. Sell your business value, not your products or services.

5. Gain relationship superiority. Recognize your personal strengths and the value you bring to the marketplace.

6. Use the measures and KPI targets as the predetermined clearly defined goals that define personal and organizational success.

7. Use the competencies to differentiate yourself. Use the competencies to define your business value. Use the competencies to focus resources on performance improvement.

8. Use the competitive analysis to obtain the intelligence required to defeat the competition.

9. Learn what your competition says about you and how they say it. Deliver inoculation messages so that the competitor loses credibility.

COMMON SALES PROBLEMS

There are five common sales problems that every Doer Seller and every professional salesperson must overcome on a regular basis. One way to look at a problem is to think of the problem as a puzzle that needs to be solved. Understanding the root cause of the problem helps solve the puzzle. Below is a simple assessment. All you need to do is put a checkmark in each box that you believe is causing the problem, and you have taken the first step in solving the puzzle.

The Problem	Root Cause of the Problem
1. Not Making Enough Outbound Calls	a. Negative attitude about making outbound (cold) calls ☐
	b. Fear of personal rejection ☐
	c. Lack of confidence in self and/or what you are selling ☐
	d. Too few quality prospects ☐
	e. Lack of sales experience or a lack of product knowledge ☐
	f. Scheduling conflicts or personal organization issues ☐
2. Not Scheduling Enough First-Time Sales Meetings	a. Not using a pre-approach business value message ☐
	b. After making contact, selling your offerings instead of the first-time meeting ☐
	c. No business value elevator pitch or phone script to follow ☐
	d. Unable to link to the contact's business issues ☐
	e. Not assertive enough to overcome objections and close for the first meeting ☐
	f. Not persistent or enthusiastic enough after making contact ☐
	g. No tactics to handle screening by the administrative assistant or to overcome leaving voice-mail messages without getting a return call ☐

The Problem	Root Cause of the Problem
3. Poor Results from a First-Time Sales Meeting	a. Lack of a compelling interactive sales presentation ☐
	b. Lack of emotional capital required to ask the tough questions ☐
	c. Lack of intellectual capital required to answer the tough questions ☐
	d. Unable to identify underlying problems/challenges that justify your solutions ☐
	e. Unable to communicate the value associated with your solution(s) ☐
4. Spending Too Much Time Pursuing Unqualified Sales Opportunities	a. Positioned too low in the prospective client's value chain ☐
	b. Frequently the prospect does not fit any Target Prospect Profile ☐
	c. The buyer's budget does not align to your company's profit margins ☐
	d. You are frequently late entering the buying process ☐
	e. You are unable to identify the buyer's pain points ☐
5. Not Winning Enough Strategic Sales Opportunities	a. Unwilling to consistently use a formal sales process designed for Complex Sales Opportunities ☐
	b. Unable to execute a Competitive Game Plan ☐
	c. Unable to effectively sell your company's business value ☐
	d. Unable to differentiate your company from the competition ☐
	e. Unable to utilize your company's internal resources to help close the deal ☐

SALES COMPETENCIES

Simply put, a competency is something that is done exceptionally well; in other words, something that is accomplished by a Doer Seller or salesperson that is above average. Every sales training company offers its own unique version of what it takes to be successful in sales, and from the seller's perspective all are correct. Sales Competencies are used for hiring, screening potential employees, and for professional development.

Below is an illustration of how I use my list of Core Sales Competencies for professional development.

> **Read the definition of each competency and rate yourself using the following scale:** 1 = Needs Improvement, 2 = Average Performance, 3 = Above Average Performance, 4 = Guru (Expert). *If you rated the competency as a 1 or 2, start working on your performance improvement Plan of Action.*

1. **Business Acumen:** Demonstrating insight into business trends. Identifying and aligning supplier offerings to a client's business objectives. Understanding the financial impact of a buying decision.

2. **Relationship Management:** Being able to establish a vision for a relationship and the ability to develop and manage that relationship. Establishing personal currency with a client contact. Being able to sustain personal credibility over time.

3. **Being Value Savvy:** The ability to translate your business language into the client's business language. The ability to sell business value instead of products and

services. The ability to align your deliverables in business terms to the client's business objectives. The ability to solve business problems for a client.

4. **Executive Bonding:** The ability to develop long-term relationships based on your understanding of the person's goals, objectives, and values. The ability to adapt to the client's corporate culture. The ability to contribute to personal and professional agendas. The ability to act as a long-range planning partner or business problem-solving counselor.

5. **Political Adeptness:** Identifying and professionally capitalizing on political forces in an organization.

6. **Competitive Differentiation:** Being able to identify a competitor's strengths and weaknesses and being able to use that information to help the competitor lose. Being able to capitalize on the business competencies that are critical from the client's perspective. Being able to identify and capitalize on those competencies that you perform exceptionally well.

7. **Resource Optimization:** The ability to manage and maximize internal and external resources to ensure sales success.

8. **Communication Effectiveness:** Being able to communicate complex ideas orally and in writing.

9. **Planning Capabilities:** Being able to make your ideas doable. The ability to think and plan strategically and the ability to execute a plan.

10. **Demand Creation:** The ability to Create Demand for a product or service by identifying, tracking, and

measuring the client's business results. Establishing a Return on Investment tracking system. Listening beyond product needs to add value to the customer's customer.

Personal Attributes that Support Sales

In addition to the Core Sales Competencies, here is a list of personal attributes that are also important. You can rate yourself using a simple "Yes" or "No" rating system.

- ❖ Adaptability
- ❖ Analytical thinking
- ❖ Creativity
- ❖ Ethicality
- ❖ Flexibility
- ❖ Innovative thinking
- ❖ Integrity
- ❖ Self-motivation
- ❖ Objectivity
- ❖ Open-mindedness
- ❖ Persistence
- ❖ Positive personal image

- ❖ Personal initiative
- ❖ Professionalism
- ❖ Reliability
- ❖ Risk taker
- ❖ Self-confidence
- ❖ Self-esteem
- ❖ Tactfulness
- ❖ Team player
- ❖ Tenacity
- ❖ Trustworthiness
- ❖ Valuing others
- ❖ Visionary thinking

Writing a Preliminary Value Proposition

One of the most challenging tasks for any Doer Seller or professional salesperson is to be able to define and then communicate an organization's business value. Writing a preliminary value proposition is a powerful way to accomplish that task. Speaking strictly from a Strategic Selling perspective, we should be able to write a preliminary value proposition that specifically targets an important account without spending a huge amount of thinking time. The key to making that happen is in being able to follow a proven process that gets results. Using the template on the next page, create several different versions of the value proposition to see which you like best. The template requires that you follow the nine steps below:

1. Name your target. (Can be an individual, specific company or business unit, or group of companies within a specific vertical market.)

2. Using your own language, describe the products and/or services you would provide to the above target. (These are your deliverables.)

3. Now translate your deliverables into a business language that an executive or functional manager would understand and appreciate. (Use the target's language, not your language.)

4. List three specific features associated with using your deliverables or organization. (A feature is a prominent aspect of something.)

5. For each feature, list one important benefit that can be obtained. (A benefit is something that aids or promotes well-being.)

6. Name two (maybe three) possible Critical Success Factors (CSFs) that are based on your research or personal knowledge and that you think are important to the above target. A CSF is a measurable criterion that is considered most vital to achieving a goal, objective, or strategy, or an area, function, or process which is highly sensitive to an organization's success or failure. CSFs are driven by different business functions and are almost always measurable. CSFs can malfunction or not meet expectations. A malfunctioning CSF is a problem that causes pain.

7. Describe one possible malfunction for each CSF above.

8. Now assume you have validated that the pain is real. Describe your solution. How would you reduce or eliminate the pain?

9. Assume the target buys your solution. Describe the outcome as a result and describe who benefits from the result. Whenever possible, use realistic measurable results.

Template—First Draft of Value Proposition

We can provide (#1 Target) with (#3 Translated Deliverables).

Results include (#5 The Benefits).

We have identified (# 6 CSFs) as areas where we can make a specific contribution. By delivering (#8 Solutions) you will obtain (# 9 Outcomes).

Please keep in mind that once you complete this planner and a rough draft of the value proposition using the template, you will need to commit time to refine (wordsmith) the final value proposition.

TIME MANAGEMENT

If you do an Internet search on "time management," you will get a lot of hits. There are books, articles, workshops, and formal training courses that you can take to help you become better at managing your time. The intent here is to get you to consciously recognize that time does not stop and realize if you do not make the right decisions concerning how you use your time, your stress levels will increase and your health and job performance will suffer. Time is like being given an allowance. Every day we get twenty-four hours of time to spend, and that is it!

To simplify a very complicated subject, I am breaking down the idea of time management into three categories. It is the last category, work time, where we spend eight to twelve hours a day, five to six days a week, expending the most energy.

Start with the 80/20 rule. You can control 80% of your time at work. The other 20% is filled with the things you cannot control: internal and external interruptions and fire fighting. So let's talk about the 80% of the time you can control.

1. Start with a prioritized list of your top six high-payoff activities. If you have a manager, share the list to get agreement. If there is disagreement, be prepared to negotiate.

2. Once the list is completed, brainstorm what you can do to spend more time in each of those activities.

The next step that is required to improve your time management skills is to identify if you own any of the most famous time killers. If you do, start working on changing the behavior. Put a checkmark in the box if you identify with the item.

- ❖ Procrastination ☐

- ❖ Poor planning skills ☐

- ❖ Working on low-priority activities before high-payoff activities ☐

- ❖ Lacking self-discipline ☐

- ❖ An inability to say "no" ☐

- ❖ Perfectionism ☐

- ❖ Not prioritizing tasks ☐

- ❖ Lacking persistence, determination, and mental toughness ☐

- ❖ Reacting to other people's misconceptions ☐

- ❖ Personal inflexibility concerning external circumstances ☐

- ❖ Personal inflexibility concerning internal circumstances ☐

In addition to identifying the most potent time killers, there are some additional rules for being successful at time management that you should be aware of.

1. Be willing to take calculated risks.

2. Become a master firefighter: (a) stay calm; (b) isolate and identify cause and effect; (c) return conditions to normal as soon as possible; (d) learn something from each crisis;

(e) implement corrective measures; and (f) document, document, document.

3. Define and live by your personal values.

4. Demonstrate personal and organizational flexibility.

5. Get really good at communicating orally and in writing.

6. In order to be focused, you need a list of written goals. Be really good at planning and executing your short-term goals and long-term objectives.

7. Know and act on the difference between "imperative" and "important."

8. Never assume anything; communicate with the people you work with.

9. Never, ever clutter your mind with trying to remember what you have to do. Use an electronic calendar (your CRM or Microsoft Outlook). Schedule everything, no matter how small. Schedule meetings, phone calls, tasks that do not require planning, projects that do require planning. *If you don't schedule time for making outbound calls to schedule sales meetings with potential clients, you won't have any sales meetings.*

10. Never worry; use a worry list.

11. Respect the time of others.

12. Set appropriate standards of excellence for yourself and for others.

13. Set time limits on completing low-priority tasks.

14. Understand that being different is not necessarily undesirable.

15. Use technology to the fullest.

16. Use productive meeting strategies; always use a written agenda.

17. When handling the flow of paper, touch the paper only once.

CHAPTER 5—UNDERSTANDING AND MANAGING THE SALES PIPELINE

Having an in-depth understanding of the functionality of a sales pipeline is the single most important behavior that any Doer Seller or salesperson must be able to demonstrate to management. In fact, it is the single most important discipline that a Doer Seller or salesperson must personally master in order to be successful in today's rapidly changing business environment. It is this belief that motivates me to offer the details of the process in a separate chapter. The phases described below can be adapted into whatever CRM system is being utilized by your company.

❖ **Phase I—Pursuit or Suspect**

  ➢ In this phase, leads can be inbound or outbound. This includes referrals, Web and telephone inquiries, RFPs and RFQs from known and unknown contacts, industry events, Webinars, marketing campaigns, and the individual effort of a Doer Seller or salesperson.

  ➢ If the contact is not in the CRM, enter the required information.

  ➢ After the seller conducts a sales meeting in person or on the phone, he or she makes a decision as to the following:

    ▪ Is the opportunity worth moving to the next phase? If not, the contact remains in the Pursuit or Suspect Phase. If it is worth pursuing, the contact moves to the Business Development Phase.

- And, if it is worth pursuing, is the opportunity Transactional or Strategic in nature?

❖ **Phase II—Business Development**

➢ If the seller decides to pursue the opportunity, the CRM is updated to Business Development.

➢ The seller uses the Probability Calculator to establish a probability percent. See page 115.

- The seller can use the answers as an Insight Tool to obtain missing information that will help improve the probability of winning the sales opportunity.

➢ The seller sends a Letter of Understanding (LOU) to validate the next steps in the sales cycle.

➢ The seller schedules a preliminary meeting with the fulfillment team to further scope the opportunity.

➢ As the seller schedules and attends additional meetings with the potential client, the CRM is updated.

➢ If the opportunity is Strategic, the seller schedules time to work on a formal sales process designed for Complex Sales.

➢ When the buyer agrees to or requests a proposal or quote, the CRM is updated to the Proposal phase.

❖ Phase III—Proposal

➢ The seller pulls the proposal team together to develop the proposal.

➢ If possible, the seller schedules a meeting with the potential client and meets with a personal Ally to deliver a "Straw Proposal" to get feedback on content and pricing before submitting the formal proposal.

➢ The seller delivers the final proposal to the potential client decision-making team and establishes a yes/no Decision Date.

➢ The seller sends a second LOU to validate delivery of the proposal and the agreed-to Decision Date.

➢ The Seller updates the probability percent using Probability Calculator.

➢ The seller follows up with the potential client before the agreed-to Decision Date to answer questions and to get feedback on the status of the proposal.

▪ If the opportunity is Strategic in nature, the seller asks probing questions about the buyer's concerns and takes proactive measures to try and close the opportunity. The seller uses the tactics associated with the formal sales process.

▪ If the opportunity is Transactional in nature, the seller will not be able to deliver a Straw Proposal and most likely will not be able to follow up to ask probing questions.

❖ **Phase IV—Won/Lost Stage**

➢ The seller obtains a decision from the potential client as to whether the opportunity was won or lost, and the CRM is updated accordingly.

➢ If the opportunity is lost, the seller should complete a Win/Loss debrief to look for patterns to gain insight on the loss. (This should be a corporate discipline that is followed without exception.)

➢ If the opportunity is won, the seller should complete a Win/Loss debrief to look for patterns. (This should be done occasionally to gain insight on selling behaviors.)

➢ The seller determines if the account is Key, Secondary, or Tertiary and updates the CRM.

▪ If the account is a Key Account, the seller determines what formal Account Management Practice will be used to Defend & Farm the account. If the account was an existing account, this step should have already been completed.

➢ After a specific period of time (determined by management), if no decision is made by the buyer, the opportunity should be closed and moved to the lost category. *Caution: Not following this discipline has a negative impact on the metrics and on the ability to accurately forecast using the active pipeline numbers.*

The Probability Calculator

The Questions	Answers	Points
I am connected to the Financial Decision Maker(s) for this sales opportunity.		
I passed inspection with the Screeners and/or End Users of my product or service.		
I have defined a Viable Solution (Product/Service, Price, and Close Date) for this sales opportunity.		
I determined there are adequate budget dollars available to support my Viable Solution.		
I determined there is enough business/personal pain to motivate the prospect to buy.		
I identified the Personal Agendas of my key contacts and am able to articulate the Wins they desire.		
I obtained meaningful competitive intelligence (how many, who they are, value chain positioning).		
I validated that our vertical market and/or project experience is competitive when compared to other vendors.		
I validated that the buyer's time requirements align with our ability to deliver.		
I have established a relationship with an Ally or Sponsor that has a high degree of influence on the decision process.		

The answers to the question and their point values are as follows:

Yes = 10 Points | No = 0 Points | Maybe = 5 Points | Don't Know = 0 Points | Not Yet = 0 Points

THE IDEA OF A WIN/LOSS DEBRIEF

The discipline of using a Win/Loss Debrief is about behavioral learning. By looking for patterns in our behavior, we capitalize on what we do right and improve on what we do wrong.

Enter Account Name:	
Enter Dollar Value:	
Enter Your Name:	
Enter Won or Lost:	
Questions	**Possible Answers**
What is or was the **Sales Cycle Timeline?**	Less Than 90 Days 3 to 12 Months Over 12 Months
How would you rate the clarity of your **Sales Objective** (what, how much, by when)?	Not Defined Started/Incomplete Clearly Defined
How would you rate your understanding of the contact's **Personal Agenda** as it relates to this potential sale?	Unknown Incomplete Clearly Defined
How would you rate your understanding of the contact's **Professional Agenda** and/or **Business Pain Points** that are motivating the sale?	Unknown Incomplete Clearly Defined
How would you rate your relationship with the **Financial Decision Maker(s)?**	Nonexistent Moderate to Weak Strong
How would you rate your relationship with the **End Users** of your product or service?	Nonexistent Moderate to Weak Strong
How would you rate your relationship with the **Screeners** of your product or service?	Nonexistent Moderate to Weak Strong

Did you have a **Personal Ally** or **Sponsor** who was or is helping you with your **Sales Objective**?	No Maybe Yes
What degree of influence do your **Primary Contacts** have on the **Final Buying Decision**?	None Low to Moderate High
What mode would you attribute to your **Primary Contacts** concerning your **Sales Objective**?	Shop for Best Price Improve Business Results Problems to Solve Grow the Business
What is or was your **Competitive Strategy**?	Price vs. Price Product vs. Product Use Industry Presence Sales and Relationship Superiority
Did the **Proposed Solution** meet the requirements of the project as defined by the client?	No Partially Yes

CHAPTER 6—THE IMPORTANCE OF DECISION RATES

The term "Closing Rate" is the one common factor that brings all sellers together across every vertical market, and it does not matter if the seller is in business-to-business sales, business-to-consumer sales, or business-to-government sales. Closing Rate is represented as a percent of the number of opportunities that were closed of the total number of opportunities that were quoted. Closing Rates vary between sellers within an organization, between the types of products and services being sold, and between different vertical markets. There are, however, Closing Rate targets that are, or at least should be, established by management. As an example, for a technology company we might look for a 50% to 65% Closing Rate. For a professional services firm, we might look for a 40% to 55% Closing Rate.

The term "Closing Rate" represents the seller's perspective. Closing Rate is about how many deals I, the seller, closed for the week, or month, or year. There is, however, another way to look at the concept which better represents the buyer's side of the equation. That is the term "Decision Rate." Decision Rate is about the techniques we use to influence the buyer into making a decision that favors the seller. This technique requires the seller to have firsthand knowledge around a specific set of questions that will allow the seller to have a positive influence on the buying decision. There are three factors that directly impact Decision Rates:

1. What is the source of the lead (inbound, outbound, or referral)?

2. Is the opportunity strategic or transactional in nature?

3. What is the level of competition for the product and/ or services being sold in the marketplace (negligible, moderate, severe)?

The following questions work best with an inbound or outbound lead that is strategic in nature, and where there is moderate to severe competition for the business. Be aware that the less information you think you can gather from a particular sales opportunity, the less qualified the opportunity. You should assess your ability to gather answers to these questions early in the sales cycle. This symbol (💣) indicates that the question is also relevant for a transactional sales opportunity.

❖ **Has the potential client been receptive to co-developing a value proposition?** To qualify, a value proposition must be written. A value proposition translates your product/service offering into the language of business. Usually, preliminary value propositions are market-segment focused. A co-developed value proposition is client focused. It is more specific. This question is about process. Have you delivered a written value proposition? Have you asked the potential client to help you make it more specific? The value proposition process is a key indicator concerning the decision making process. Will this be a Best Value decision or a Best Price decision?

❖ **What is driving the potential client's decision to buy?** The more information you have concerning why the client wants to buy, the easier it is to differentiate yourself. This question is about linking prime buying motives. Why does the executive want to buy? Why does the functional manager want to buy? Simply put, the more you know about why people want to buy and the higher that knowledge goes in the value chain, the better off you are. 💣

❖ **What business result does the potential client seek from your solution?** What will they have that they don't have now? What benefit will they gain? What loss will they avoid? 💣

❖ **What financial measures surround the delivery of the solution?** This question concerns Return on Investment.

❖ **Are there any geographic challenges associated with delivering this solution?** Will delivering your product/service increase cost? Will delivering your product/service erode margins? 💣

❖ **What is the timeframe for delivery of the solution?** Do you know the drop-dead date? For example, if it doesn't happen by a certain date, it won't happen at all. Do you know when a final decision will be made? 💣

❖ **Is there adequate funding available for this project?** How much is budgeted for the project? 💣

❖ **Are there any delivery or service challenges associated with this deal?** Will you have difficulty in delivering your intellectual property? 💣

❖ **Can the potential client handle this project without a struggle?** If the potential client has no experience in doing an implementation of this magnitude, then they will struggle—for example, an enterprise-wide implementation of a new software package. The answer to this question points to client satisfaction issues and could lead to cost overruns. 💣

❖ **Can your company make money on this deal?** If you answered yes, how do you know? What test is used to validate the pricing? If you answered no, get management approval to continue working on the deal. If you do not know, talk to management. 💣

❖ **Will winning this deal add value to your position in the marketplace?** Will this potential client's name help you win additional business in a particular sector? Will it add prestige to your client list? Will it give you more credibility? 💣

❖ **Can you differentiate your solution from the competitor's solution?** Can you capitalize on strengths the competitor does not have?

❖ **Can the competitor differentiate their solution from your solution?** Can the competitor capitalize on strengths you do not have?

❖ **What is your company's history in this account?** You either have a history or you do not. If you do, what is the history? Did things go well or were there problems? Sometimes there is a history, and the seller doesn't know the history because they did not reach out to other team members. 💣

❖ **What is the incumbent's history in the account?** How high is the incumbent positioned in the value chain? How long has it been doing business with the client? Were there any problems in the past?

❖ **Can your corporate culture align or adapt to the potential client's corporate culture?** Corporate culture is defined as "language, behavior, and symbolism." Is there anything in your corporate culture that might conflict with the potential client's corporate culture? For example, your profit margins are measured in dollars and the client's are measured in cents. *How about the incumbent or another competitor?*

❖ **Are you early in the buying process?** Is there an incumbent? Has a competitor already submitted a proposal? Are you the first to submit a proposal or answer an RFP? Are you the first or last to present your ideas to a committee? *How about the incumbent or another competitor?* 💣

❖ **Do you know who is influencing the buying decision from behind the scenes?** If so, what is your relationship with that person? How much do you know about the informal buying process? How much do you know about the formal buying process? In both cases, who are the Primary Sponsors? Do you have relationships with these people? *How about the incumbent or another competitor?*

❖ **Have you identified and aligned to your contact's professional and personal agendas?** Do you know what your contacts would like to achieve professionally and/or personally? If you do, have you demonstrated how you can help them achieve their goals and objectives? *How about the incumbent or another competitor?*

❖ **Do you have an executive-level Sponsor?** *How about the incumbent or another competitor?* 💣

Consider the above questions as a qualification encyclopedia. The more you know, the better positioned you are to make decisions on sales strategy and tactics. The more you know, the better positioned you are to close the sale. The more you know, the easier it is to manage your time. The less you know, the higher the risk of losing to the competition! Be objective, stand back, and ask yourself this question: *based on my current relationships and position in the account, how much information can I really uncover before the client makes a buying decision?*

APPENDIX A—INSIGHT TOOLS AND SALES PLANNERS

An Insight Tool is designed to do just what it describes: offer insight to the person using the tool. An Insight Tool is also designed from a practical application perspective and is quick and easy to use. Insight Tools are used electronically, that is, with a computer.

Sales Planners, on the other hand, are printed documents. Sales Planners are designed for creative thinking and force the user to allocate time to think through the process, the theory being that writing crystallizes thinking. Sales Planners tend to generate amplified outcomes when they are facilitated in a team environment where people can share their intellectual capital.

Performance Management Practices

Insight Tools

1. **Annual Pipeline Planner Simulator (Excel):** Used by sellers at the beginning of the year to complete their revenue forecast based on previous years' statistics. The tool has four worksheets: (1) Pipeline Forecast; (2) Pipeline Simulator; (3) Business Development vs. Existing Business; (4) Time Priorities.

2. **Business Development Assessment (Word):** A series of twenty-two questions that, when rated, allow the seller and his or her manager to work on improving selling skills required for new business development.

3. **Probability Calculator (Excel):** Objective tool used to determine the probability of winning a specific sales opportunity. When this tool is utilized by an entire sales team, there is increased forecasting reliability from the sales pipeline.

4. **Monthly Calculator (Excel):** Calculator helps sellers determine what they must accomplish in a given month to stay on target with an annual quota. The calculator uses actual statistics to determine activity requirements.

5. **Quarterly Calculator (Excel):** Calculator helps sellers determine what they must accomplish during a quarter to stay on target with an annual quota. The calculator uses actual statistics to determine activity requirements.

6. **Sales Pipeline (Excel)**: Tool that can be used as an active pipeline if there is no CRM. This tool can also be used as a model to setup a CRM system. The tool includes a Forecast Tab that tracks progress on KPIs, informs the seller about what needs to be accomplished to manage the pipeline toward an annual quota, and offers a Win Rate and Probability Percent forecast.

7. **Sales Process Win/Loss Debrief (Excel):** Behavior learning tool used to learn why a seller wins and/or loses a specific sales opportunity. When used consistently, shows selling behaviors that impact winning and losing sales opportunities.

Sales Planners

8. **CPAS, or Co-developed Performance Appraisal System (Word):** Formal performance appraisal system that offers both objective and subjective viewpoints. CPAS is designed to be used on a quarterly basis.

9. **CPAS Skills Test:** Two sets of questions around new business development and sales. The questions are co-answered by the seller and his or her manager and are used to set quarterly professional development goals as a part of the CPAS process.

Competitive Practices

Insight Tools

10. **Competitive Game Plan Tool (Word):** Assists in developing a value-driven competitive strategy around the core competencies of an organization. Assesses applicability based on the seller's rating, the competition's rating, and significance to the buyer of each competency. This tool requires customization.

Sales Planners

11. **Worksheet Competitive Analysis (Word):** Used to identify core competencies and to build a glossary of terms that defines each core competency.

Account Management Practices

Insight Tools

12. **Account Ratings—Stars (Excel):** Used when evaluating several Key Accounts to prioritize the investment of time.

13. **Key Account Selector (Excel):** Used by anyone who owns multiple accounts to objectively identify the status of each account as Key, Secondary, or Tertiary.

14. **Account Action Plan (Excel):** Used by the account management team to identify contact's position in the value chain, political rating, sales impact, the seller's objective, and the appropriate action step. The tool is designed to manage five accounts where the selling organization has a major presence.

15. **Key Account Test (Excel):** Ten questions that determine if an individual should invest time in completing a KASP or SOAP Account Planner.

Sales Planners

16. **KASP, or Key Account Sales Plan (Word):** Formal account planner used to Defend & Farm the Key Accounts within a specific vertical market. Two versions of the KASP are available: one for a single Key Account (ten pages) and one version for four different Key Accounts (twenty-four pages).

17. **SOAP, or Strategic Ownership Account Plan (Word):** Formal account planner used to Defend & Farm a single strategically important Key Account. SOAP is designed as a fast, bottom-line account management process based on a political capital worksheet and six strategic positioning questions (six pages).

New Business Development Practices

Insight Tools

18. **Master Point System (Excel):** The tool looks at thirteen steps of business development and assigns a point value to each step. There is a worksheet for planning the year and worksheet for each month, January to December.

The goal worksheet tracks points earned monthly, the dollar value of each point based on YTD sales, time spent of sales YTD, and percent of annual points earned YTD. The rates worksheet tracks Meeting Conversion Rates and Decision (Closing) Rates.

19. **Monthly Plan of Action (Excel):** Used by business developers to establish must-do monthly activity requirements based on a quota and specific performance statistics.

20. **Preliminary Value Proposition (Excel):** Automated tool that actually writes a rough draft of a preliminary value proposition based on how the user answers specific questions about a client's need or vertical market.

21. **Scorecards for Telephone Prospectors and Business Developers (Excel):** Used to track activity and results based on weekly goals. Also, generates reliable performance statistics.

Sales Planners

22. **Ideal Client Profile (Word):** Used to identify common factors from three highest-revenue-generating clients around sixteen different account characteristics.

23. **Sales Meeting Debrief (Word):** Used to track progress around a formal complex sales methodology.

Strategic Selling Practices

Insight Tools

24. **Master Fast Track (Excel):** Identifies Strategic Sales Objective, Tactical Sales Objective, sales timeline,

twelve-question knowledge audit, and relationship audit. This tool includes an action step page. Completion of all the worksheets takes between twelve and fifteen minutes.

25. **Knowledge Audit (Word):** Twenty-five questions that identify missing information. Scoring is broken down into five categories: Opportunity Score, Value Score, Political Score, Competitive Score, and Business Forecast as Highly Vulnerable, Threatened, and Secure.

26. **Win/Loss Debrief (Excel):** Twelve questions used to determine the patterns of why a seller wins and/or loses specific sales opportunities.

27. **Qualifying Questions (Word):** Used to qualify a sales opportunity early in the sales cycle around four areas of concern: sales basics, political capital, relationships, and competitive strategy.

28. **Strategic Selling Test (Excel):** Ten questions that quickly determine if the seller should invest time in using a formal sales process. Scoring indicates if the end user should not invest time in a formal sales process, should use Master Fast Track, or should invest time using a Deal Pursuit Sales Plan.

Sales Planners

29. **Deal Pursuit Sales Plan Workbook (Word):** Formal sales planner that includes a Knowledge Audit, Relationship Audit, and action steps around implementing a value, political, and competitive strategy. The workbook is fifteen pages and is used to pursue complex sales opportunities.

APPENDIX B—END-USER ROADMAP FOR SUCCESS

I will imagine for the moment that you read this book and are ready to make a decision concerning what you can use that will help you perform the Doer Seller role more effectively, with less stress. To help facilitate the takeaway process, I make the following recommendations. Consider this an end-user roadmap for success.

1. Have a positive attitude and capitalize on that attitude on a daily basis.

2. Understand what motivates you personally and seek to understand what motivates your existing clients and potential clients.

3. Fall in love with your work, find your passion, and nurture that passion.

4. Do not allow worries to dominate your thinking; use a worry list.

5. Define your role in each of the five Sales Management Practices and get agreement from management. If you are on your own, review the roles with someone you trust.

    a. Formalize what you will measure and how often you will track and report your results. Write your own job description and negotiate agreement with your superiors. If you are your own boss, write the job description anyway.

    b. Prepare in advance a Competitive Game Plan for your most dangerous competitors. Use the Game Plan often when pursing strategically important accounts.

    c. Decide what formal Account Management process you will use, and use it when appropriate.

    d. Develop a New Business Development Plan of Action in writing, and follow the plan.

    e. Decide what formal Strategic Selling process you will use, and use it when appropriate.

6. Internalize the significance of each of the four Sales Opportunity Practices and use the knowledge to gain market share.

7. Define in writing the five to seven best sales ideas (see chapter 4) and implement a Plan of Action to utilize those ideas for your own personal benefit.

8. Make sales pipeline management a way of life. Use your company's CRM or use an Excel version of the sales pipeline.

9. Focus on your Decision Rate, not your Closing Rate, and make that an ongoing goal for continuous performance improvement.

10. Save time and avoid missteps. Be self-disciplined. Use those Insight Tools and Sales Planners that give you the most confidence and consistent results.

GLOSSARY OF TERMS

In the world of information technology, a common language is used to standardize how different applications talk to each other so they can communicate more efficiently and more effectively. In business, a common language is a cultural system, used to standardize how employees with different backgrounds and different job functions can communicate more efficiently and more effectively.

We have discussed the five Sales Management Practices and the four Sales Opportunity Practices in great detail. By adopting the language associated with those concepts, we can impact how we think and how we behave, and hopefully become more efficient and more effective.

Using a common sales language is especially important when we are dealing with organizations with several locations across the United States and the globe. Different cultures impact sales results in varying ways.

Attitude: A habit of thinking usually reflected in one's behavior which has been programmed over time by family, friends, and life and work experiences.

Attributes: Defined as a set of qualities owned by an individual. For example: trustworthiness, self-confidence, professionalism, personal initiative, and analytical thinking.

Business Acumen: The knowledge of and understanding of business issues in regard to the impact of profit, growth, and shareholder value. The ability to gain insight about important business issues by interacting with businesspeople in their work environment. Included is the ability to make quick, accurate judgments about critical business issues with a high degree of accuracy.

Business Function: A commercial or industrial enterprise can be broken down into separate business functions that, when viewed together, represent the whole enterprise. Sales and Marketing, Finance, Human Resources, Research and Development (R&D), Quality Control, Customer Satisfaction, and Information Technology are all business functions. Responsibilities are those actions and activities assigned to or required or expected of a person or group within a business function that require work time to achieve the goals and/or objectives of that business function.

Client: One that purchases the professional advice, service, support, and knowledge of another. The term is primarily used in business-to-business sales.

Cold Calling: A telemarketing process using an interactive phone script. Cold calling is primarily used in business-to-consumer sales.

Communication Effectiveness: The ability to communicate complex ideas orally and in writing and the ability to simplify complex ideas so people with different backgrounds can easily understand them. Included is the ability to differentiate what is most meaningful to a specific audience from an abundance of information.

Competitive Differentiation: The ability to demonstrate how the strengths of your products or services differ from those of the competition and the ability to use competitive game plans as a means of achieving competitive differentiation.

Complex Sale: A sales cycle lasting three months to a year where multiple decision makers control the buying process.

Core Competencies: A set of required skills and a foundation of knowledge that allow an organization to perform a particular business function. For an organization, core competencies can encompass a set of global skills, qualities (characteristics), and business processes. In a competitive business environment, competencies are the core engine that drives competitive advantage. There are two types of core competencies, current and emerging.

Create Demand: When the seller engages a buyer in solving an existing problem that remained unresolved over a period of months or years. When the seller identifies a need the buyer didn't realize he or she had and can engage the buyer in co-developing a solution. When the seller uncovers the buyer's pain and can relieve, reduce, or eliminate the pain using the seller's offerings.

Critical Success Factors (CSFs): Specific issues considered most vital to the achievement of organizational strategy or the area most sensitive to the organization's success or failure. CSFs are usually identified by an analysis of the organization's internal strengths and weaknesses and external environmental opportunities and threats. CSFs can relate to a positioning statement, mission statement, or strategic concept. CSFs are also referred to as Root Drivers.

Customer: One that purchases a product or service as a commodity. The term is primarily used in business-to-consumer sales.

Decision Analysis (DA): An analysis to select a preferred action after a problem analysis. DA usually includes reviewing alternative decisions and their consequences.

Defend & Farm: When the account management team defends the account from competitive encroachment and continues to expand their reach within the account to grow profitable revenue streams in other business units and geographic locations, and when the account management team is able to generate revenue from other products and services not previously delivered within the account.

Doer Seller: A Doer Seller is any individual within any vertical market in any size company who is expected to deliver a quality product or service, or is expected to manage a group of people or manage a business practice, while being given a sales goal or quota and being expected to deliver the revenue dollars associated with that goal or quota in a timely manner along with his or her other responsibilities.

Driving Force: Is the single strategic area which determines and drives the organization's total strategic concept. Driving force can dictate future products and markets. Driving force describes the most critical business dimension that, if attacked by a competitor, could destroy the business enterprise.

Executive Bonding: The ability to establish long-term relationships without regard to the outcome of a sales campaign, including the formation of a personal or professional relationship, especially through frequent and ongoing contact.

Forecast: An anticipated or predicted result as in a revenue forecast or sales forecast. Forecasts are usually built on reliable historical data.

Goal: A short-term (one year or less), specific, measurable, attainable, realistic, and where the action steps are at least 51% controllable by the person setting the goal.

Govern: To bring into conformity using rules or principles as to how people behave, and to direct or strongly influence the behavior of others.

Inoculation Message: A preemptive selling tactic in which one party attempts to foresee and neutralize potentially damaging criticism from another party by being the first to confront troublesome issues such as an organization's weaknesses. Primarily a psychological approach when making statements during a conversation that is intended to be subliminal (below the threshold of conscious perception).

Key Performance Indicators (KPIs): Measurements of human or organizational performance. For management, KPIs are barometers to individual and organizational success.

Long-Range Planning: A process based on current operations into the future. Usually set in financial terms, long-range plans emanate from the lowest levels where information is readily available.

Motivation: The reason or purpose that people take action. Motivation can be negative or positive in nature.

Muddle: Uncertainty and confusion, which is most often caused by a lack of clearly defined goals.

Objective: A long-term (over one year), specific, measurable, attainable, realistic, and where the action steps are at least 51% controllable by the person setting the goal.

Opportunity: Something that is prized, desired, or needed; can be controlled or influenced; and is external to the organization.

Organization Development: Activities that improve organizational performance.

Organization Performance: The efficiency and effectiveness with which an organization implements its strategy.

Plan of Action: A specific plan of support of a goal or objective that includes obstacles, solutions, rewards, action steps, required internal/external resources, and target dates.

Planning Expertise: The act or process of making or carrying out plans; more specifically, the establishment of goals, policies, and procedures for a business plan or sales plan. Planning expertise requires disciplined thinking and a commitment to understanding the principles of time management.

Political Adeptness: Being highly proficient in understanding the theory and practice of how people influence others in a business environment, including who is involved in power plays and power struggles.

Problem: Deviation from a value, norm, standard, goal, objective, mission, quest, or strategic concept.

Problem Analysis (PA): The analysis of the root cause of a problem and potential alternative solutions.

Project: A one-time goal or objective, as opposed to a continuously monitored primary goal or objective.

Prospect: A potential buyer, customer, or client.

Quest: An internal reward-driven statement that obtains an emotional response. A quest can be used as a motivational tool for a group of individuals (employee eyes only).

Relationship Management: The ongoing management of relationships in a complex business environment. Relationship management implies that one or more parties manage trust, honesty, and integrity as part of the process.

Resource Optimization: The ability to manage internal and external resources (assets, people, events, corporate skills, proprietary knowledge, and business practices), including those of the selling and buying organizations, during a sales pursuit, and the ability to manage those resources during the delivery phase of the sale. Also includes the ability to leverage political influence or insights into business trends, issues, or Critical Success Factors.

Root Driver: A measurable criterion that is considered most vital to achieving a goal, objective, or strategy, or an area, function, or process which is highly sensitive to an organization's success or failure.

Satisfy Demand: When a buyer continues to purchase a product or service from the seller as the preferred vendor.

Service Demand: When the buyer is looking for a solution to a problem, has no relationship with an incumbent, and encourages many vendors to bid on the business. When the buyer is looking for a solution to a problem, one has a working relationship with an incumbent but decides to replace incumbent because they are dissatisfied. When the buyer is looking for a solution to a problem and is forced by a mandate to get competitive bids or wants to leverage the bids to get the lowest price.

Situational Analysis (SWOT): An assessment of the strengths and weaknesses internal to the organization and the opportunities and threats external to the organization. The process also includes identifying those factors that can be controlled or influenced and those factors that are uncontrollable.

Strategic Concept Statement (SCS): A word picture or visualization of the nine strategic dimensions describing what the organization will look like at some future point in time. Used by employees as a decision-making tool. Having a clear strategy is essential to the organization's fundamental sense of purpose.

Strategic Dimensions: The nine business areas most common to all business enterprises. Taken together with the selection of Driving Force, they define and form the conceptual framework of an organization's strategy. They include: (1) Products/Services Offered, (2) Market Needs, (3) Technological Capabilities, (4) Production Capabilities, (5) Method of Sale, (6) Method of Distribution, (7) Natural/Supplier Resources, (8) Size/Growth, and (9) Return/Profit.

Strategic Thinking: The ability to clearly visualize a future outcome and the ability to map each step backwards from the desired outcome to the current point in time.

Strategic Timeframe: The period of time over which a particular strategic concept will dictate decision-making, planning, and execution.

Strategy: The framework which guides both the nature and direction of the organization, or the framework that guides both the nature and direction of a sales campaign.

Strengths: Internal organizational characteristics offering potential advantages in the pursuit of the strategic concept.

Success: The progressive realization of worthwhile predetermined personal goals (inside or outside the workplace). Success can also be defined as the achievement of a strategic concept, mission, or quest within a specific timeframe.

Tactics: A plan, strategy, or set of action steps used during a campaign (political or sales campaign).

Talking Points: A technique used by a seller during a sales meeting to link the corporate competencies of the seller's company to the needs of a buyer based on their position in the value chain. Talking points are based on the contact's job focus, area of responsibility, and professional and personal concerns based on current market conditions.

Threats: Potential obstacles to the realization of the organization's strategic concept. Threats are derived from the external environment. Threats can be influenced or they are not controllable.

Value Added: A feature that is price driven and profit sensitive and represents a company's willingness to deliver more to the customer than the customer expects until added value becomes the expectation.

Value Redefinition: Value redefinition is the ability to discover and deliver business value to a customer. Value redefinition requires the conversion and communication of a product/service description into a business solutions description. Value redefinition connects a vendor's competencies as solutions to the customer's Critical Success Factors in business terms.

Values: The principles, standards, and qualities considered worthwhile that serve as the foundation from which an organization develops and aligns its corporate strategy with its operational planning and management tactics. Values serve as unifying principles at all levels of the organization and guide human behavior and day-to-day decision making concerning interactions with the internal and external stakeholders.

Weaknesses: Internal organizational characteristics offering potential disadvantages during the pursuit of the strategic concept.

Win Rate: Reflects the total effort of the seller in using corporate resources to make sales and is primarily used for revenue forecasting. Win rate is the % of total dollars sold compared to the total value of the pipeline which includes dollars sold, dollars lost, and dollars still active (business development & proposals).

21866769R00087

Made in the USA
Middletown, DE
13 July 2015